COMFORT FOOD FAST

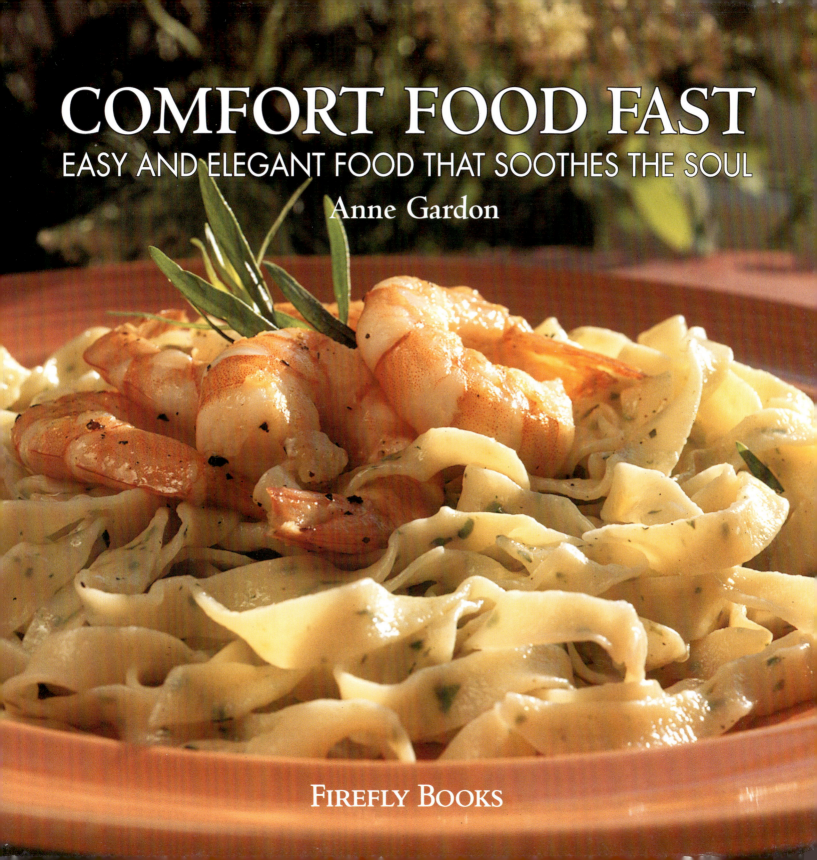

COMFORT FOOD FAST

EASY AND ELEGANT FOOD THAT SOOTHES THE SOUL

Anne Gardon

FIREFLY BOOKS

A FIREFLY BOOK

Published by Firefly Books Ltd. 2001

First Printing 2001

U.S. Cataloging-in-Publication Data
(Library of Congress Standards)

Gardon, Anne.
  Comfort food fast : easy and elegant fare that soothes the soul / Anne Gardon. – 1st ed.
[176] p. ; col. ill. : cm.
Includes index.
Summary: Recipes for hearty dishes, chunky soups and stews, and old-fashioned desserts
ISBN 1-55209-595-9 (pbk.)
1. Entrées (Cookery). 2. Desserts. 3. Cookery. I. Title.
641.8 21 2001 CIP

Published in the United States in 2001 by
Firefly Books (U.S.) Inc.
P.O. Box 1338, Ellicott Station
Buffalo, New York 14205

Produced by
Bookmakers Press Inc.
12 Pine Street
Kingston, Ontario K7K 1W1
(613) 549-4347
tcread@sympatico.ca

Design by
Janice McLean

Printed and bound in Canada by
Friesens
Altona, Manitoba

Printed on acid-free paper

National Library of Canada Cataloguing in Publication Data

Gardon, Anne
  Comfort food fast : easy and elegant fare that soothes the soul

Includes index.
ISBN 1-55209-595-9

1. Quick and easy cookery. I. Title.

TX833.5.G37 2001   641.5'55   C2001-930454-4

Published in Canada in 2001 by
Firefly Books Ltd.
3680 Victoria Park Avenue
Willowdale, Ontario M2H 3K1

The Publisher acknowledges the financial support of the Government of Canada through the Book Publishing Industry Development Program for its publishing activities.

DEDICATION

This book is dedicated, with much love and care, to all gourmets who are fond of Grandma's cooking but would enjoy it even more if it were updated and simplified.

CONTENTS

INTRODUCTION

What does "comfort food" mean to me? Naturally, it means hearty dishes, thick, chunky soups, meaty stews and old-fashioned desserts. But more important, it means tastes that I know. After all, what's more comforting than well-known and much-loved dishes, flavors familiar to your palate and smells full of good memories—a favorite pizza, a pie straight out of your childhood? I wanted to share my fondest memories here, so I have included many recipes from my native Provence.

To me, comfort also means not spending my time fussing in the kitchen while my guests are having fun in the dining room. So in this book, there are no soufflés ready to collapse, no hollandaise sauce that might curdle at the last minute, no elaborate arrangements. Instead, there are lots of one-pot meals you can serve straight from the oven.

Getting Comfortable

If you have to spend an hour or more cooking, why not make it an enjoyable and learning experience? Here are a few of the secrets I've acquired over the years.

When a lot of peeling or cutting is required, get your feet off the ground. Sit on a stool or a chair. If you have to stand at the stove for a long time, a soft rubber mat underfoot offers a little extra comfort.

While preparing food, listen to your favorite CD or radio program. Sip a glass of wine or juice or a cup of tea. While cooking, study the chemistry of food, paying attention to the interactions and reactions of your ingredients and to their changes in texture and consistency. It's a good way to understand the process, and it will make you a better cook. In other words, treat cooking like a hobby. You will have a lot more fun.

About My Cooking

I call my cooking CHEF's Cuisine (Cheap, Healthy, Easy and Fun). I don't believe you need to spend a lot of money to eat well. And by eating well, I'm referring to gourmet meals as well as health food.

Ingredients

The best, always! I grow lots of vegetables organically, and many—such as carrots, parsnips, squash and sunchokes—are intended for winter storage. I use them in all kinds of recipes throughout the year, from appetizers to desserts. As you will see, I am especially fond of the squash family.

Today, you can find fruits and vegetables from around the world, fish from every sea, meat from every edible animal (even ostrich), specialty coffees, fine cheeses and gourmet condiments at your neighborhood food mart. The global supermarket! Nevertheless, in this book I have stayed away from exotic ingredients as much as possible. So you should have no trouble making my recipes even if you live in the boondocks, as I do.

Tastes are very subjective. You may like cooked endives, which I hate with a passion, and you may not be as fond of parsnips as I am. To accommodate our differences, I've added one or more variations to most recipes, including meatless options for the vegetarians in your family.

Tools of the Trade

I cook for a living, but I am not a professional chef. I have seen chefs at work, however. They slice, chop, dice, beat or knead with just elbow grease. Because I don't have their dexterity, speed or precision, I have bought or been given many "power tools" over the years—mixer, blender, food processor, gadgets—with which to grind, slice, crush and beat food into submission. And I must admit, I enjoy the power of my electric friends.

Here are some of the tools I've found helpful in the kitchen:

KitchenAid®. It gets the least use, but it does the hardest work: beating egg whites, mixing pastry, kneading bread dough. You can do without it, if you have an electric mixer and a food processor.

Food processor. It chops and mixes and makes silky pasta and pizza dough, biscuits, muffins. A must!

Blender. A must as well, if you want really creamy soups, frothy drinks, smooth vinaigrettes and instant mayonnaise.

Electric mixer. Mine comes with various accessories, even a bowl to chop herbs, although it doesn't do a good job of that. The herbs tend to waltz around with the blades and get bruised rather than chopped.

Mini-chop. This is my tool of choice for chopping anything dry—herbs, spices, nuts. It is inexpensive and well worth having. You can also use a coffee grinder if it is reserved for just that purpose.

Pressure cooker. Not an electrical appliance but a "power tool" nonetheless. I wouldn't live without one. For quick comfort, it is unbeatable. Pressure cookers not only reduce cooking time drastically but also preserve nutrients and keep meat tender and juicy. A blessing!

Crockery

Besides regular pots and pans of various sizes, I have a French ceramic glazed cast-iron pot for slow-simmering stews. I can cook up to eight portions of chicken cacciatore in it for freezing. For smaller portions—up to four—I use Corning® Ware. Although I am fond of the look and feel of earthenware and love the taste of food cooked in it, dishes in modern ceramic are so easy to use—from the fridge to the stovetop or the oven—and easy to clean too. The results are delicious, and they look terrific on the table as well.

Quick Comfort From the Freezer

Nothing beats a freezer for quick comfort. My freezer serves two functions: It is a cold pantry with frozen vegetables, fruits, crêpes, pie shells, puff pastry and many other ingredients just waiting for my inspiration; and it is a gourmet shop, where I often stop when I have no time to cook. The menu is quite extensive: borscht, phyllo rolls, chicken cacciatore, lamb stew, sauces, cakes.

I freeze meals in individual portions in airtight freezer bags (the air is removed using a straw) or in plastic containers. I label all packages with names and dates and use them within a few weeks or months.

About the Pictures in This Book

The food shots are true to life. I took them—yes, I did!—in my kitchen and dining room. The food was prepared following the exact instructions and cooking times that appear in these recipes. The dishes were photographed as they came out of the pot, pan or oven. Here and there, I arranged vegetables for an attractive appearance and searched for the most photogenic angle, but I never used any trick, shortcut in cooking or foreign substance to make the dish look more appealing. And after the shooting, I always ate my subject.

   Now, it is all in your hands: my favorite recipes of old, my latest creations, my personal gardening tips...and my hope that you have as much pleasure cooking and eating well as I have.

   Bon appétit!

Scottish Oat Scones, page 180

ON THE LIGHT SIDE

Phyllo Triangles, page 24

DILL, POTATO AND SALTED COD SALAD

As an appetizer or a light lunch and even for a picnic, this salad offers comfort throughout the seasons.

1 lb.	salted cod	500 g
4	large potatoes, unpeeled	4
½ cup	olive oil	125 mL
	Salt and pepper	
½ cup	chopped fresh dill	125 mL

Soak the cod overnight in cold water. Rinse and poach for 5 minutes in simmering water. Drain the cod, flake with a fork, and set aside.

Cook the potatoes in boiling salted water until done. Peel, and cut into slices.

Heat ¼ cup (60 mL) of the oil in a heavy skillet, add the potatoes, season lightly with salt and pepper, and cook, turning, over medium heat until golden on both sides. Remove from the pan with a slotted spoon, and set aside. Add the remaining ¼ cup (60 mL) oil, and cook the cod for 2 to 3 minutes until crisp.

To serve, gently mix the cod with the potatoes and dill. Or arrange the potato slices in a circle on serving plates, spoon the cod in the center, and sprinkle with dill. Serve warm.

Serves 4

BEAN AND CILANTRO SALAD

Tasty, filling and nutritious, this salad is a complete meal, summer or winter.

	Olive oil	
2	red bell peppers, cut into cubes	2
1	zucchini or yellow crookneck summer squash, cut into cubes	1
2	15-oz. (425 mL) cans black beans	2
2	green onions, minced	2
½ cup	chopped fresh cilantro	125 mL
	Grated peel and juice of 1 lime	
	Salt and pepper	
	Tabasco sauce	

Heat about 2 Tbsp. (30 mL) oil in a skillet, and cook the red peppers over high heat until the skin starts to brown. Using a slotted spoon, remove the peppers from the skillet, and set aside.

In the same skillet, cook the zucchini or squash over medium heat for 2 to 3 minutes. Cover, remove from the heat, and let stand for 5 minutes.

Meanwhile, drain and rinse the beans. In a large bowl, combine the red peppers, zucchini or squash, beans, green onions, cilantro and lime peel and juice. Season with salt and pepper to taste, drizzle with oil and add a dash of Tabasco sauce. Stir gently, then let stand for 1 to 2 hours before serving.

Serves 4-6

Prepared in a jiffy, fritters make a quick and easy lunch. Usually, they are deep-fried, but I prefer to cook fritters in a nonstick pan with just a little oil. (This avoids the smell that tends to linger in the house after deep-frying.)

CORN FRITTERS

1 cup	canned corn, drained, or frozen corn, thawed	250 mL
2	eggs, separated	2
2 Tbsp.	all-purpose flour	30 mL
	Salt and pepper	
	Olive oil	
	Rock salt	
	Chopped mixed fresh herbs (thyme, oregano, marjoram)	

Mix together the corn, egg yolks and flour. Season with salt and pepper to taste. Beat the egg whites until stiff, then fold them into the corn mixture.

Heat a little oil in a nonstick pan. Drop in tablespoonfuls of corn batter, and fry over medium-high heat, turning, until the fritters are golden on both sides. Drain on paper towels. Sprinkle with rock salt and herbs, and serve.

Makes about 8 fritters

VARIATION: Replace corn with grated carrots; add 2 Tbsp. (30 mL) heavy cream or yogurt.

MUSHROOM STRUDEL

This light and flaky strudel can be prepared ahead of time and frozen, uncooked or partially cooked. Do not thaw before baking.

	Olive oil	
2 cups	sliced mushrooms	500 mL
2 cups	chopped leeks, white part only	500 mL
½ cup	ricotta, cottage or goat cheese	125 mL
1	egg	1
	Salt and pepper	
1 tsp.	dried herbs	5 mL
1 tsp.	breadcrumbs	5 mL
1 tsp.	chopped fresh parsley	5 mL
4	phyllo pastry sheets	4

Heat 1 Tbsp. (15 mL) oil in a pan, and cook the mushrooms over medium heat until golden. Remove the mushrooms with a slotted spoon, and set aside.

Add more oil, if necessary, and cook the leeks for about 5 minutes, until softened.

In a medium bowl, combine the mushrooms, leeks, cheese and egg, season with salt and pepper to taste, and mix well.

In a small bowl, mix together the dried herbs, breadcrumbs and parsley.

Preheat the oven to 400°F (200°C).

Work with one sheet of phyllo at a time, and keep the remaining pastry under a damp tea towel to prevent drying. Spread one sheet on a completely dry work surface, brush with oil, and sprinkle with one-quarter of the breadcrumb mixture. Place another sheet on top, and brush with oil. Place half of the cheese filling at the narrow end of the sheets,

leaving 1 inch (2.5 cm) on each side. Roll once, tuck in sides, and roll up. Place on a greased baking sheet. Repeat with the remaining phyllo pastry sheets.

Brush the top with oil, and sprinkle with the remaining breadcrumb mixture. Place the baking sheet in the center of the oven, lower the oven temperature to 375°F (190°C), and bake for 25 minutes. Let cool slightly, cut each strudel in half, and serve with salsa, homemade ketchup or Romesco Sauce (page 114).

Serves 4-6

Phyllo pastry

I always have a package of phyllo pastry sheets in the freezer. I make rolls, strudels, bundles, triangles and finger food with them, everything from appetizers to desserts.

When preparing rolls—kale, feta cheese and roasted-tomato pesto is my favorite stuffing—I always make a dozen or more and freeze the extras. When I want a quick lunch, I just pop the frozen rolls in a 400°F (200°C) oven for 25 minutes. If I do not use the whole package of phyllo, I refreeze the remaining pastry for another time.

Phyllo pastry has many uses and always produces spectacular results.

TIP: Work with one sheet of phyllo pastry at a time, covering the remaining pastry with a damp cloth or plastic wrap to prevent drying. Freeze on a cookie sheet lined with waxed paper, then transfer to a rigid container. Use within a few weeks for best results. No need to defrost before baking at 375°F (190°C) until golden, about 20 minutes.

AUMONIÈRES

Aumonières are "little bundles." Stuffed with vegetables, meat or seafood, they make an elegant first course. When in a rush, I prepare them with a medley of spring or summer vegetables (page 84). Try the Mushroom Strudel filling (page 22) for tasty little bundles.

Spread one sheet of phyllo pastry on a dry work surface, brush with olive oil, and sprinkle with the breadcrumb mixture. Cover with another sheet. Cut into four squares. Place about 3 Tbsp. (45 mL) filling in the center of each square. Bring sides up to form a bundle. Place on a nonstick baking sheet. Bake at 375°F (190°C) for 15 minutes, until golden.

CAPONATA PIE

Spread one sheet of phyllo pastry on a dry work surface, brush with olive oil, sprinkle with the breadcrumb mixture (see Mushroom Strudel, page 22). Repeat until you have three sheets of pastry, one on top of the other. Line a large round or rectangular pie plate with the pastry. Fill with Caponata (page 90), sprinkle with grated Parmesan cheese, and bake at 375°F (190°C) for 20 minutes. Serve warm.

Serves 4-6

NOTE: For a sweet version of this pie, see Quick Apple Pie (page 158).

CHOUX PASTRY

Just as versatile as crêpes, these light puffs freeze well and can be thawed in the oven in minutes, to become decadent profiteroles or delightful appetizers when stuffed with salmon mousse, cheese or other savory fillings.

2 cups	water	500 mL
½ cup	butter	125 mL
1 tsp.	salt	5 mL
2 cups	all-purpose flour	500 mL
8	eggs, plus 1 optional egg to brush on top	8

In a heavy saucepan, combine the water, butter and salt. Bring to a boil. Add the flour all at once, and stir with a wooden spoon until the mixture forms a ball. Remove from the heat, and add the eggs, one at a time. Use an electric mixer for this "muscled" task. Beat the dough until it is smooth and elastic.

Drop spoonfuls of dough onto a well-greased cookie sheet, brush with a beaten egg, if desired, for a shiny finish, and bake at 375°F (190°C) for 35 to 40 minutes. With a sharp knife, pierce each puff to allow the steam to escape, and let the puffs cool in the oven, with the door open.

Puffs can be frozen in rigid containers; separate layers with waxed paper before freezing. To reheat, do not thaw. Bake at 350°F (180°C) for 10 minutes.

Makes about 3 dozen puffs

GOUGÈRE NIÇOISE

A gougère is a cheese-flavored choux pastry. In Burgundy, it is served during a winetasting.

PASTRY

1 cup	water	250 mL
¼ cup	butter	60 mL
1 Tbsp.	salt	15 mL
1 cup	all-purpose flour	250 mL
4	eggs	4
1 cup	grated Gruyère, Emmenthaler or Cheddar cheese	250 mL

GARNISH

Olive oil

1	onion, minced	1
1	red bell pepper, cut into strips	1
1	small eggplant, cubed	1
4	ripe tomatoes, peeled and coarsely chopped	4
	Salt and pepper	
¼ cup	minced fresh basil leaves	60 mL

TO MAKE PASTRY: In a heavy saucepan, combine the water, butter and salt. Bring to a boil. Add the flour all at once, and stir with a wooden spoon until the mixture forms a ball. Remove from the heat, and add the eggs, one at a time. Use an electric mixer for this "muscle" task. Beat until the dough is smooth and elastic. Add the cheese, and mix well.

Spoon the dough in a large circle or in four individual circles on a greased baking sheet. Bake at 375°F (190°C) for 35 to 40 minutes, until golden. With a sharp knife, pierce the pastry in several places to allow the steam to escape, and let it cool in the oven, with the door open.

TO MAKE GARNISH: Heat 2 Tbsp. (30 mL) oil in a skillet, and cook the onion for 2 minutes, until soft. Add the red pepper, and cook for 1 minute, then add the eggplant and tomatoes. Season with salt and pepper to taste, cover and simmer for 15 to 20 minutes.

Spoon the vegetables into the middle of the gougère. Sprinkle with the basil, and drizzle with oil.

Serves 4-6

TOMATO-BASIL PASTE

I make all kinds of tasty light meals with tomato-basil paste, which I prepare and freeze in quantity when tomatoes are in season. The amount of tomatoes and basil used is totally subjective, depending on your own taste and on the availability of the ingredients.

Choose ripe, firm tomatoes. Italian, or plum, tomatoes are best, but any tomato with thick walls will do. Halve the tomatoes, or if they are large, cut them into quarters, and place, skin side down, on a baking sheet lined with aluminum foil, as the acid from the tomatoes will corrode the finish of the baking sheet.

Sprinkle with salt, and bake at 300°F (150°C) for 4 hours, until the tomatoes are shriveled but not dry.

Loosely fill the bowl of a food processor with fresh basil leaves, and pulse to chop. Add enough baked-tomato pieces to fill the bowl halfway. Puree at high speed. Then, while processing at low speed, add enough olive oil to make a smooth paste. Season with salt and pepper to taste.

Line ramekins or small custard cups with plastic wrap, fill each with the tomato-basil paste, fold plastic wrap over, and freeze. Unmold the bundles when frozen, and store in the freezer in dated plastic freezer bags for up to six months.

MINUTE PIZZA

Spread a large pita bread with Tomato-Basil Paste (page 30), then garnish with pepperoni slices, ham and artichoke hearts, if desired. Cover generously with grated mozzarella, sprinkle with your choice of herbs, and bake at 375°F (190°C) for 20 minutes, until the cheese is melted.

AVOCADO SANDWICH

Cut a 9-inch (23 cm) piece of baguette in half lengthwise, and spread with a generous layer of Tomato-Basil Paste (page 30). Garnish with avocado slices, season with salt and pepper to taste, drizzle with olive oil, and enjoy. You may also add lettuce, tomato and cucumber slices.

SOUPS

Creamy Soup, page 40

LIGHT GARLIC SOUP

A sound piece of advice for anyone suffering from a cold is: Drink plenty of fluids. And this soup is exactly the kind of fluid you should drink. To speed recovery, double the amount of garlic—or triple it, if you dare. But don't go on a first date the following day or plan an intimate dinner.

3 Tbsp.	olive oil	45 mL
4	garlic cloves, minced	4
4 cups	chicken stock	1 L
	Croutons	
	Grated Parmesan cheese	

Heat the oil in a large saucepan, stir in the garlic, and cook for just a few seconds. Add the stock, and bring to a boil. Reduce to medium heat, and cook for 5 minutes.

To serve, garnish with croutons and cheese. Or toast French bread, arrange the slices in the bottom of the serving bowl, cover with grated Cheddar or Gruyère cheese, and ladle the soup over.

Serves 4

VARIATIONS

❧ Beat 2 eggs, and stir into the hot soup. Cook over medium heat, stirring gently, until egg filaments form.

❧ Garnish each serving with a poached egg.

❧ For color, add 2 tomatoes, peeled, seeded and chopped.

CURRIED PARSNIP AND PEAR SOUP

I love parsnips. Rich in potassium and vitamin C, they are sweet and creamy, ideal for desserts and soups and anything in between.

2 Tbsp.	butter	30 mL
1	large onion, minced	1
	Curry powder (see Note below)	
3 cups	chicken stock	750 mL
1 cup	chopped, peeled parsnips	250 mL
	Salt and pepper	
1	pear, peeled and chopped	1

Melt the butter in a heavy saucepan, add the onion, and cook over medium heat for 1 minute, until soft.

Stir in the curry powder to taste, and cook for 30 seconds. Add the stock, parsnips and salt and pepper to taste. Cover and simmer for 20 minutes. Puree the soup in a blender with the pear, reheat for a few seconds, if necessary, and serve.

Serves 4

NOTE: The amount of curry powder can vary according to your taste and the type of curry powder you use.

VARIATIONS ON A CREAMY SOUP

I make a variety of creamy soups using the ingredients I have on hand. Sometimes, I combine two or more vegetables; sometimes, I use only one vegetable and add herbs or spices. Here are a few combinations that work especially well:

- carrot and parsnip
- sweet potato and celery root
- butternut squash with ground ginger
- carrot with cumin

Sauté 1 onion in a little vegetable oil or butter, add 2 cups (500 mL) or more cubed raw vegetables and 3 to 4 cups (750 mL–1 L) chicken stock. Cook until the vegetables are tender, add herbs or spices to taste, if using, then puree with an immersion mixer or in a blender.

If the soup is too thick, thin with some milk or light cream. If it is too thin, reduce the soup to the desired consistency over medium-high heat.

Serves 4

CHESTNUT SOUP

Highly nutritious and energy-rich, chestnuts are the perfect winter food. They are delicious braised with Brussels sprouts or sautéed in butter and served as a garnish for poultry and game. They are also wonderful in stuffings and soups, such as this delectable offering. Chestnuts come from the chestnut tree and are not to be confused with water chestnuts, which are the tubers of an aquatic plant from Southeast Asia.

2 Tbsp.	olive oil	30 mL
1	onion, minced	1
1	celery stalk, chopped	1
1	potato, peeled and cubed	1
2 cups	chicken stock	500 mL
1	10-oz. (284 mL) can chestnuts in water	1
	Salt and pepper	
	Heavy cream	

In a heavy saucepan, heat the oil, then add the onion and cook for 1 minute, until soft. Add the celery, potato and stock. Bring to a boil, reduce heat, and simmer for 20 minutes.

Puree the soup in a blender with the chestnuts and their soaking water. Return to the pan. Season with salt and pepper to taste, and simmer for 5 minutes.

Garnish each serving with a swirl of cream.

Serves 4

SUNCHOKE AND CHEDDAR SOUP

The sharpness of old Cheddar adds punch to the subtle flavor of sunchokes. If fresh sunchokes (Jerusalem artichokes) are not available, use canned artichoke bottoms.

2 cups	cubed, peeled sunchokes	500 mL
	(about 1⅓ lb./600g)	
2 Tbsp.	butter	30 mL
2 Tbsp.	all-purpose flour	30 mL
1 cup	milk	250 mL
	Salt and pepper	
1 cup	grated old Cheddar cheese	250 mL

Cook the sunchokes in 2 cups (500 mL) boiling water until tender. Drain and set aside, reserving the cooking liquid.

Melt the butter in a heavy saucepan, sprinkle with the flour, and cook, stirring, for 1 minute. Add the reserved cooking liquid and the milk, and season with salt and pepper to taste. Cook over medium heat, stirring constantly, until thickened, about 5 minutes.

Combine the white sauce and the sunchokes in the bowl of a blender, and puree until creamy. Return to the pan, add the cheese, and cook over low heat, stirring until cheese is melted.

Serves 4

Sunchokes

Also called a Jerusalem artichoke, this tasty tuber is not an artichoke at all but a member of the sunflower family. *Helianthus tuberosus*, a North American perennial, grows mainly in the eastern half of the continent. It is very invasive and is therefore not recommended for a small garden. Growing up to nine feet (3 m) tall, the sunchoke is an excellent windbreak. And each plant can easily yield 40 pounds (18 kg) of tubers.

Delicious when stir-fried in olive oil with fresh herbs, baked in a Tian (page 89) or grated and served raw, sunchokes have fewer calories than potatoes and are rich in vitamins A and B complex, potassium and phosphorus. They also contain inulin, a sugar similar to insulin, making them a wise dietary choice for diabetics and hypoglycemics.

LENTIL SOUP

I soak lentils and other pulses in water for at least two days so that they start to germinate, which makes them more nutritious and more digestible. Sprouted legumes also cook more rapidly. While 3½ ounces (100 g) of dried lentils contain no vitamin C, the same amount soaked in water for 40 hours contains 69 milligrams of vitamin C.

1 cup	dried lentils	250 mL
	Olive oil	
1	onion, minced	1
1	leek, white part only, minced	1
1	celery stalk, chopped	1
1	carrot, diced	1
2	garlic cloves, crushed	2
1	bay leaf	1
4 cups	chicken stock	1 L
	Salt and pepper	
	Chopped fresh parsley	

Soak the lentils in cold water overnight or longer, changing the water twice a day. Drain.

In a heavy saucepan, heat 2 Tbsp. (30 mL) oil, and cook onion and leek over medium heat, stirring, until soft, about 3 minutes.

Add lentils, celery, carrot, garlic, bay leaf and stock. Season with salt and pepper to taste. Bring to a boil, then reduce heat and simmer until lentils are cooked, about 45 minutes. Sprinkle with parsley and drizzle with oil before serving.

Serves 4-6

VARIATION: Any dried beans can be substituted for the lentils. Or use canned beans or lentils: Cook the vegetables in the stock until tender, then add drained canned beans or lentils and reheat.

WHITE BEAN AND SAVORY SOUP

Although I prefer to use dry pulses, I always have a few cans of beans in my cupboard—black beans, broad beans, kidney beans, chickpeas, flageolets, black-eyed peas—for quick soups, salads and side dishes. This hearty soup uses canned beans.

2 Tbsp.	olive oil	30 mL
1	onion, minced	1
1	19-oz. (540 mL) can white beans, drained	1
2 cups	chicken stock	500 mL
2 Tbsp.	fresh summer savory, or 1 Tbsp. (15 mL) dried	30 mL
	Salt and pepper	
	Croutons (optional)	

In a heavy saucepan, heat the oil, and cook the onion for 1 minute, until soft. Add the beans, stock and savory. Season with salt and pepper to taste, and cook over medium heat for 15 minutes. Puree the soup in a blender or with an immersion mixer. Sprinkle with croutons, if desired, and serve.

Serves 2-3

HEARTY SOUP FROM SCRATCH

You can make soup with whatever is at hand, provided you have a few canned goods and some fresh vegetables. The basics are the same, no matter what the ingredients. For eye appeal, combine different-colored vegetables. Orzo, a small rice-shaped pasta, is available in Italian grocery stores.

	Olive oil	
1	onion, minced	1
2	chorizo sausages	2
1 cup	diced squash	250 mL
2	leeks, white part only, sliced	2
1	sweet potato, diced	1
1 cup	beet greens, cooked	250 mL
1	19-oz. (540 mL) can black-eyed peas, drained	1
1	12-oz. (341 mL) can kernel corn, drained	1
1	10-oz. (284 mL) can beef stock	1
2 cups	coarsely chopped stewed tomatoes	500 mL
3 cups	water	750 mL
1	small chili pepper	1
	Salt and pepper	
1 cup	orzo	250 mL
	Chopped fresh cilantro (optional)	

In a large pot, heat a little oil, and cook the onion for 1 minute. Add all the remaining ingredients except the orzo, and season with salt and pepper to taste. Bring to a boil, then simmer for 20 minutes. Add the orzo, and cook until the pasta is tender. Remove the chili pepper and discard. Before serving, sprinkle with cilantro, if desired. This soup freezes well.

Serves 6-8

VARIATIONS: Replace the orzo with rice, use another type of bean or sausage, add celery or green peas... use your imagination. By omitting the sausages, you can create a vegetarian delight.

BORSCHT

Like all chunky soups, this one freezes well and will comfort you in the heart of winter.

3 Tbsp.	olive oil	45 mL
5	onions, minced	5
5	beets, peeled and cubed	5
5	potatoes, peeled and cubed	5
¾ lb.	smoked pork shank	375 g
⅓ lb.	kielbasa (Polish sausage), sliced	150 g
4 cups	shredded red cabbage	1 L
2	carrots, peeled and sliced	2
6 cups	water	1.5 L
1 Tbsp.	cumin seeds, crushed	15 mL
4	cloves	4
1 tsp.	allspice	5 mL
1	star anise	1
	Salt and pepper	
	Sour cream (optional)	

In a large stockpot or a pressure cooker, heat the oil, and cook the onions over medium heat until soft. Add the remaining ingredients, and season with salt and pepper to taste. Bring to a boil, then reduce heat and simmer for 1½ hours (30 minutes in a pressure cooker), until vegetables are tender. Remove pork shank and discard the skin and bones. Shred meat and return to soup. Top each serving with a dollop of sour cream, if desired.

Serves 8-10

SOBRONADE

Serve this hearty soup, a specialty of Périgord, a province of France, with Corn Fritters (page 21) or focaccia (page 136) and a salad for a complete meal. To make the soup for today, use canned beans instead of dried, adding them 15 minutes before the end of the cooking time. The choice of vegetables is yours—add or substitute broccoli, turnips, sweet potatoes, leeks or others—but keep the celery root, as it gives this soup its special flavor.

1 cup	dried white beans	250 mL
1 Tbsp.	olive oil	15 mL
4	slices bacon, chopped	4
1 cup	cubed smoked ham or smoked pork	250 mL
1	celery root, cubed	1
2	onions, coarsely chopped	2
2	potatoes, cubed	2
4	carrots, cut into chunks	4
3	whole garlic cloves	3
1 Tbsp.	dried herb mix	15 mL
6 cups	water	1.5 L
1 Tbsp.	salt	15 mL

Soak the beans in water for 12 to 24 hours, changing the water twice a day.

In a large stockpot or a pressure cooker, heat the oil, and cook the bacon for 1 minute. Add the ham or pork, and cook for 2 minutes over medium-high heat. Add the remaining ingredients. Bring to a boil, then simmer for 1 hour (20 minutes in a pressure cooker).

Serves 6-8

PASTAS AND GRAINS

Fettuccine à la Gigi, page 58

FETTUCCINE À LA GIGI

Gigi, a very good friend of mine, gave me this recipe. The name is not patented, however, so you may call it whatever you wish. It's a wonderful summertime dish, when fresh peas and basil (if you're making your own pesto) are abundant.

4	slices smoked ham	4
1 cup	peas, fresh or frozen	250 mL
2 Tbsp.	olive oil	30 mL
1	garlic clove, minced	1
1 cup	coarsely chopped, peeled, seeded tomatoes	250 mL
	Salt and pepper	
1 Tbsp.	pesto (optional)	15 mL
	Fettuccine for 4 servings	
	Grated Parmesan cheese	

Cut the ham into strips, and set aside. Cook the peas in boiling water for 2 minutes—they should remain crisp—drain and set aside.

In a large saucepan, heat the oil, and cook the garlic for 1 minute. Add the ham, peas and tomatoes. Season with salt and pepper to taste. Bring to a boil, then simmer, uncovered, until the sauce is thick, about 5 minutes. Stir in the pesto, if using.

Meanwhile, cook the fettuccine in boiling salted water. Drain. Add to the sauce and toss. Sprinkle with cheese and serve.

Serves 4

Homemade pasta

Making your own fresh pasta is easy, and the delicate, tender noodles beat dried pasta every time. You don't even need a pasta machine. You can roll out the dough with a rolling pin. The basic recipe calls for 1 large egg and 1 Tbsp. (15 mL) olive oil per 1 cup (250 mL) flour, with salt to taste and enough cold water to make a dough. The amount of water depends on the type and dryness of the flour.

The ideal flour is Italian semolina, which is made from durum wheat. Pale yellow in color, it gives the best texture and flavor to the pasta. Unfortunately, it is not readily available. All-purpose flour will do almost as well. For a golden hue, replace about one-quarter of the white flour with corn flour. For color and taste, you can also substitute pureed vegetables—squash, carrot, spinach—for the water.

TARRAGON FETTUCCINE

Tarragon is a hardy perennial with delicate foliage. Mine grows in a flowerbed among chives and black-eyed Susans. I harvest the leaves throughout the growing season and freeze them. To freeze tarragon, pick tender young shoots in the morning or the evening. Wash, if necessary, and pat dry, then separate leaves from stalks, and place in a freezer bag.

2 cups	all-purpose flour	500 mL
1 tsp.	salt	5 mL
¼ cup	chopped fresh tarragon leaves	60 mL
2	large eggs	2
2 Tbsp.	olive oil	30 mL
	Grated Parmesan cheese	

BY HAND: Combine the flour, salt and tarragon in a large bowl, and make a well in the center. In a small bowl, beat together the eggs, oil and about 2 Tbsp. (30 mL) cold water, and pour the mixture into the well. Mix ingredients together with a fork, then with your hands, adding more cold water as needed, 1 Tbsp. (15 mL) at a time. Knead the dough until smooth and elastic, about 5 minutes.

IN A FOOD PROCESSOR: Combine all the ingredients except the cheese, and mix until a ball forms. Knead until smooth and elastic. The dough should not be sticky.

Chill the dough for 1 hour. Roll the dough out to the desired thickness, and cut the pasta into fettuccine noodles using a sharp knife or a pasta machine.

Bring a large pot of salted water to a boil, and cook fettuccine until al dente. A couple of minutes should be enough. Drain. Sprinkle with cheese. Serve with cooked shrimp, if desired.

Serves 4

CANNELLONI WITH RICOTTA AND SUMMER SAVORY FILLING

FILLING

2 Tbsp.	olive oil	30 mL
2	onions, minced	2
1 cup	ricotta cheese	250 mL
1 cup	cubed cooked squash (see Note below); reserve 1 cup (250 mL) cooking liquid for sauce	250 mL
2 Tbsp.	finely chopped fresh summer savory	30 mL
	Salt and pepper	
1	recipe squash pasta dough (see page 64)	1

SAUCE

2 Tbsp.	butter	30 mL
2 Tbsp.	all-purpose flour	30 mL
	Reserved cooking liquid from squash	
1 cup	light cream or milk	250 mL
1 Tbsp.	finely chopped fresh summer savory	15 mL
	Salt and pepper	

TO MAKE FILLING: Heat the oil, and cook the onions over moderate heat until soft, about 2 minutes. Combine with the ricotta cheese, squash and savory. Season with salt and pepper to taste, and mix well.

Roll out the pasta dough to desired thickness, and cut into 5-inch (12 cm) squares. Divide filling among squares, roll into tubular shapes, and place in a greased baking dish.

TO MAKE SAUCE: In a small saucepan, melt the butter, sprinkle with the flour, and cook, stirring, for 2 minutes. Add the reserved cooking liquid, cream or milk and savory. Season with salt and pepper to taste. Cook over medium heat, stirring constantly, until thick. Pour sauce over cannelloni. Bake at 375°F (190°C) for 20 minutes.

Serves 4-6

NOTE: The fastest way to cook squash is in the microwave. Peel squash, cut into cubes, and place in a microwave-safe dish. Add 2 Tbsp. (30 mL) water, cover, and cook on high until soft, 3 to 4 minutes. The cubed squash can also be boiled or steamed for about 10 minutes.

SQUASH RAVIOLI WITH CHICKEN FILLING

Winter squash, such as butternut, acorn, ambercup and pumpkin, are marvelous vegetables. They grow without fuss in well-manured soil (well-aged horse manure is best) and need watering only during dry spells. They keep for months in a cool, dry place—ideally, a root cellar or a basement, but a garage will do as long as it doesn't freeze in winter. And squash are especially rich in vitamin A.

SQUASH PASTA DOUGH

1 cup	cooked butternut squash	250 mL
2	eggs	2
2 Tbsp.	olive oil	30 mL
1 tsp.	salt	5 mL
2½ cups	all-purpose flour	625 mL

FILLING

	Olive oil	
1	onion, finely chopped	1
1 lb.	ground chicken or turkey	500 g
2 Tbsp.	minced fresh basil	30 mL
1 Tbsp.	heavy cream or yogurt	15 mL
	Salt and pepper	

TO MAKE SQUASH PASTA DOUGH: With a food processor, beat together the squash, eggs, oil and salt. Add flour until the dough forms a ball. Knead for 2 to 3 minutes. Chill for 1 hour. If making the pasta by hand, see instructions on pages 59 and 61.

TO MAKE FILLING: Heat about 1 Tbsp. (15 mL) oil in a skillet, and cook the onion until it is soft. Add the chicken or turkey, and cook over medium heat, stirring, until the meat turns white. Transfer to a bowl, and stir in the basil and cream or yogurt. Season with salt and pepper to taste.

Roll out the dough in a thin sheet. Place tablespoonfuls of the filling on the dough at regular intervals, and cover with another thin sheet of dough. Press around the fillings, then cut out individual ravioli with a pasta cutter. If you like ravioli, you may want to invest in a ravioli mold that can make a dozen or more ravioli at a time. Spread the ravioli on a floured surface, and cover until ready to cook.

Bring a large pot of salted water to a boil, add ravioli a dozen at a time, and cook until they rise to the surface. Remove with a slotted spoon, and keep warm while cooking the remaining ravioli. Serve with a chunky fresh tomato sauce, a white cheesy sauce or the sauce in the recipe for Cannelloni With Ricotta (page 62).

Makes about 3 dozen ravioli

CHAIN-COOKING LASAGNA

I prepare lasagna about three times a year—all in late August when juicy ripe tomatoes and fresh herbs are plentiful. Only three times a year? Yes, but I make six lasagna dishes at a time (my oven won't hold any more) and freeze them. It doesn't take much longer to prepare six lasagna than it does one, and my freezer fills up nicely. For convenience and best results, I use the ready-bake lasagna, which does not need to be precooked.

Exact quantities are not important in this recipe, and the ingredients can be changed to suit individual tastes. You can add meat and/or mushrooms to the tomato sauce or replace the white sauce with cottage cheese. A good tomato sauce is a must, though, so make it with sun-ripened tomatoes and fresh herbs. The sauce should not be too thick, and you will need at least 6 cups (1.5 L).

While the tomato sauce is simmering, prepare about 4 cups (1 L) of white sauce using ½ cup (125 mL) butter, ½ cup (125 mL) all-purpose flour, 4 cups (1 L) milk and 1 Tbsp. (15 mL) or more salt. Combine with 2 to 3 cups (500-750 mL) chopped cooked greens (kale, spinach, beet greens or Swiss chard). Season with salt and pepper to taste.

Arrange six 4-by-8-inch aluminum baking dishes on a baking sheet. Spread some tomato sauce in the bottom of each, cover with dry pasta and a thick layer of the white-sauce mixture. Add more tomato sauce, pasta, white sauce, and so on, to the top. Finish with tomato sauce. Cover with aluminum foil, and bake at 375°F (190°C) for 20 minutes. Let cool, then freeze. If you want to serve one lasagna right away, sprinkle the top with freshly grated mozzarella, Cheddar or Parmesan cheese, and extend cooking time to 40 minutes.

To serve frozen lasagna, thaw at least partially, then bake at 375°F (190°C) until heated through, 30 to 65 minutes. Sprinkle with freshly grated cheese, and place lasagna under the broiler for a couple of minutes until the top is golden.

Each lasagna serves 2-3

PASTA TIMBALE

Nourishing yet light, this Sicilian specialty is the perfect comfort food for summer.

WHITE SAUCE

¼ cup	butter	60 mL
¼ cup	all-purpose flour	60 mL
3 cups	milk	750 mL
	Salt and pepper	

1 lb.	vermicelli	500 g
½ cup	chopped ham	125 mL
½ cup	grated old Cheddar cheese	125 mL
½ cup	grated Emmenthaler or Gruyère cheese	125 mL
½ cup	ricotta cheese	125 mL
½ cup	grated Parmesan cheese	125 mL
½ cup	breadcrumbs	125 mL
	Olive oil	

TO MAKE WHITE SAUCE: Melt the butter in a heavy saucepan, add the flour, and stir until bubbly. Whisk in the milk, and cook over medium heat, stirring, until thick, about 15 minutes. Season with salt and pepper to taste, and set sauce aside.

Cook the pasta in boiling salted water until al dente. Drain, and toss with half of the white sauce. Set aside, and let cool slightly. Combine the ham and cheeses with the remaining white sauce, and mix well. Set aside.

Butter a 10-inch (3 L) springform pan. Dust the bottom and sides with ¼ cup (60 mL) of the breadcrumbs.

When the pasta is cool enough, wet your hands and line the prepared pan with three-quarters of the vermicelli mixture, pressing it against the bottom and about halfway up the sides. Fill the center with the ham-and-cheese mixture. Top with the remaining vermicelli.

Sprinkle with the remaining ¼ cup (60 mL) breadcrumbs, drizzle with oil, and bake at 350°F (180°C) for 50 to 60 minutes, until golden. Let cool for 15 minutes before removing the sides of the pan.

Serve with Romesco Sauce (page 114), homemade ketchup or salsa.

Serves 6-8

VARIATIONS

🌿 If you have vegetarians in your family, replace the ham with green peas or with 1 cup (250 mL) sliced mushrooms lightly sautéed in butter.

🌿 Substitute a nice soft goat cheese for the ricotta; Romano or Padana for the Parmesan; and Fontina for the Emmenthaler.

Polenta

Made from cornmeal, polenta is a traditional dish of northern Italy. Rediscovered by modern chefs, this once "peasant" food is popular again. You can buy it ready-made, in the shape of a thick sausage, but why spend the money when it is so easy to prepare from scratch? And, like pasta, polenta is so versatile!

BASIC POLENTA

4 cups	water	1 L
1 Tbsp.	salt	15 mL
1 cup	cornmeal	250 mL
	(see Note below)	

In a large saucepan, heat the water and salt until small bubbles start to rise from the bottom. Immediately whisk in the cornmeal, and bring to a boil, stirring constantly. Adding the cornmeal before the water comes to a boil will prevent lumps from forming.

Reduce the heat to medium, and cook, stirring with a wooden spoon, until the spoon can stand by itself in the mixture, 8 to 10 minutes. Pour into a greased loaf pan or a square baking dish, preferably glass. Smooth the top with a spatula, cover with foil or plastic wrap, and let cool. The polenta is then ready to be used in a variety of recipes.

The polenta can also be served hot from the stove with a hearty meat dish such as Chicken Cacciatore (page 108) or Beef Provençale (page 129). Ladle the polenta onto a serving plate, drizzle with olive oil, and sprinkle with grated Parmesan cheese. Season with pesto, if desired.

Polenta slices are delicious fried in olive oil, sprinkled with dried herbs and served as a side dish with lamb shanks (page 124).

Or arrange polenta slices in a baking dish, dot with butter, sprinkle with grated cheese, and bake at 350°F (180°C) for 15 minutes. Place under the broiler for a few minutes before serving.

Serves 4-6

NOTE: There are three different grades of cornmeal: fine, medium and coarse. Use medium for the best results.

POPIZZA

This pizza features a polenta crust, which is much more fragile than a traditional crust. When eating it, you might want to use a knife and fork rather than your hands.

Make one Basic Polenta recipe (page 71), adding 2 Tbsp. (30 mL) dried herbs during the cooking process. Spread the polenta ¾ inch (2 cm) thick on a cookie sheet, and let cool slightly.

Top the polenta with tomato sauce, sliced green peppers and mushrooms, and sprinkle generously with mozzarella cheese and fresh herbs.

Bake at 375°F (190°C) for about 15 minutes, until golden.

Serves 4-6

POLENTA AND EGGPLANT PARMIGIANA

Here is one quick and easy way to use polenta loaf.

1	eggplant	1
	Olive oil	
8	½-inch (1 cm) slices polenta loaf	8
	Salt and pepper	
2 cups	tomato sauce	500 mL
1 cup	grated Gruyère or mozzarella cheese	250 mL
	Chopped fresh herbs	

Cut the eggplant into thin slices. In a large skillet, fry the eggplant in oil until browned on both sides.

Brush a baking dish with oil, arrange one layer of polenta slices in the dish, cover with the eggplant slices, then the remaining polenta. Season with salt and pepper to taste. Pour tomato sauce over the top, and sprinkle with the cheese.

Bake at 375°F (190°C) for 20 to 30 minutes. Place under the broiler for a few minutes, until the top is brown. Garnish with herbs and serve.

Serves 2-4

BARLEY AU GRATIN

Using leftovers is one way of having comfort rapidly, and making leftovers on purpose is one way of getting ready for comfort. With this in mind, I always cook more barley, rice or wheat than a recipe calls for so that I can prepare this creamy gratin the next day.

4 cups	grated raw squash, carrots or sweet potatoes	1 L
3	eggs	3
½ cup	heavy cream or sour cream	125 mL
1 tsp.	dried herbs	5 mL
2 cups	cooked barley, wheat or rice	500 mL
	Salt and pepper	
½ cup	breadcrumbs	125 mL
½ cup	grated Parmesan cheese	125 mL
	Butter	

Combine the vegetable, eggs, cream, herbs and barley, wheat or rice. Mix well, and season with salt and pepper to taste. Pour into a well-greased baking dish.

In a small bowl, mix the breadcrumbs with the cheese. Sprinkle over the top, and dot with butter.

Bake at 375°F (190°C) for 30 minutes. Place under the broiler for a couple of minutes, until the top is golden.

Serves 4-6

MAINLY VEGETABLES

LEEK AND CHÈVRE QUICHE

If you do not like goat cheese (chèvre), you can use sharp Cheddar or Fontina, a delicately nutty cheese from northern Italy.

2 Tbsp.	butter	30 mL
3	leeks, white part only, sliced	3
1 Tbsp.	all-purpose flour	15 mL
1	pie shell	1
2 oz.	creamy goat cheese	50 g
2	eggs	2
½ cup	light cream	125 mL
	Salt and pepper	

In a large skillet, melt the butter, and cook the leeks over moderate heat for 5 minutes, until just soft. Sprinkle with the flour and toss. Spoon the leeks into the pie shell.

In a small bowl, whisk together the cheese, eggs and cream. Season with salt and pepper to taste, and pour over leeks.

Bake at 375°F (190°C) for 35 minutes, or until the top is golden and firm to the touch.

Serves 4-6

CURRIED CAULIFLOWER

This fragrant cauliflower is a perfect side dish for Charlotte With Apples and Pork (page 119), or serve it as a light lunch with steamed rice. It freezes very well.

1	large cauliflower	1
3 Tbsp.	butter	45 mL
2	medium onions, coarsely chopped	2
1 Tbsp.	curry powder	15 mL
1 Tbsp.	cumin seeds, crushed	15 mL
1 Tbsp.	brown sugar	15 mL
½ Tbsp.	salt	8 mL
1 cup	seedless raisins	250 mL
1 cup	slivered almonds	250 mL
1½-2 cups	chicken stock	375-500 mL

Separate the cauliflower into small florets. Set aside.

In a heavy pot, melt the butter and cook the onions over medium heat until soft, about 2 minutes. Sprinkle with the curry powder, stir and cook for 1 minute. Add the cauliflower and the remaining ingredients. Bring to a boil, then cover and simmer for 10 minutes, until the cauliflower is cooked but still crunchy.

Serves 6-8

MEDLEY OF SUMMER VEGETABLES WITH LINGUINE

These crisp vegetables are a great garnish for gougère.

1	red bell pepper	1
1	zucchini	1
1	carrot	1
6	asparagus stalks, or 1 small fennel bulb	6
	Olive oil	
¼ cup	pine nuts (optional)	60 mL
	Linguine for 4 portions	
	(about 8 oz./250 g)	
	Salt and pepper	
	Grated Parmesan cheese	
	Chopped fresh marjoram	

Cut the red pepper, zucchini and carrot into strips. Cut the asparagus diagonally into 1-inch (2.5 cm) sections, or cut the fennel into thin slices.

Heat 2 Tbsp. (30 mL) oil in a heavy skillet, and cook the red pepper for 1 minute over medium heat. Add the remaining vegetables and the pine nuts, if using. Stir-fry for 1 to 2 minutes, cover, turn off the heat, and let stand until the vegetables are cooked but still crisp-tender, about 3 minutes.

Meanwhile, cook the pasta in boiling salted water, drain, and toss with the vegetables. Season with salt and pepper to taste. Drizzle with oil, and sprinkle with cheese and marjoram.

Serves 4

VARIATION: You can make all kinds of vegetable mixes. Here is a spring vegetable mix using equal amounts of kohlrabi, young zucchini (crookneck or pattypan summer squash) and snow peas with fresh lemon basil.

Peel the kohlrabi, and cut into large chunks. Cut the zucchini into chunks, and cut the snow peas in half.

Melt some butter or olive oil in a large skillet, and cook the vegetables over medium heat for 2 to 3 minutes. Add a few tablespoonfuls of white vermouth or water. Season with salt and pepper to taste, cover and simmer for a few minutes, until the vegetables are cooked but still crisp-tender. Toss with chopped lemon basil.

This freezes very well, so make lots to capture the spring flavors.

VEGETABLE MEDLEY, INDIAN-STYLE

This dish goes well with grilled lamb and also makes a light lunch, with rice and grilled plantain. It is ideal for freezing.

1 cup	seedless raisins	250 mL
1 tsp.	cumin seeds	5 mL
1 tsp.	coriander seeds	5 mL
2 Tbsp.	butter	30 mL
2 Tbsp.	olive oil	30 mL
4	onions, minced	4
6	carrots, peeled and sliced	6
4	celery stalks, chopped	4
1 tsp.	brown sugar	5 mL
	Salt and pepper	

Soak the raisins in ½ cup (125 mL) warm water for 10 to 15 minutes, until soft. Drain and set aside. With a mortar and pestle, grind the cumin and coriander seeds together.

In a large skillet, heat the butter and oil. Cook the onions over medium heat until soft, about 2 minutes. Add the ground cumin and coriander, and stir for 30 seconds. Add the carrots, celery, raisins, brown sugar and salt and pepper to taste. Cover and simmer for 15 minutes.

Serves 4-6

VARIATION: Add 2 cups (500 mL) cooked chickpeas or other beans.

TIAN

Tian is both the name of an earthenware ovenproof dish from Provence and the kind of gratin meal cooked in it. In winter, it can be made with any type of root vegetables, such as celery root, potatoes, turnips and sweet potatoes. In summer, try a colorful mix of bright red tomatoes, vibrant yellow crookneck summer squash and deep green zucchini (the summer blend is baked, uncovered, for only 20 minutes).

1	onion, minced	1
1	small celery root	1
½	butternut squash, neck part only	½
¼ cup	olive oil	60 mL
½ cup	water or white wine	125 mL
½ tsp.	salt	2 mL
2 Tbsp.	dried herb mix	30 mL
1 Tbsp.	warm honey	15 mL

Spread the onion in a baking dish. Peel the celery root, cut in half lengthwise and then into ¼-inch-thick (6 mm) half-moon slices. Peel the squash, and slice like the celery root.

Arrange rows of celery root and squash over the onion. In a small bowl, mix the oil and water or wine, and pour over the vegetables. Sprinkle with the salt and herbs. Cover and bake at 375°F (190°C) for 30 minutes or longer, depending on how crisp or tender you like your vegetables. (To prepare this dish in advance, simply reduce the cooking time to 20 minutes so that the vegetables won't be too soft when reheated.)

Drizzle the honey over the top, and broil for 5 minutes.

Serves 6-8

CAPONATA AND RATATOUILLE

These wonderful vegetable stews are from the Mediterranean basin: Caponata (without zucchini) from Sicily; Ratatouille (with zucchini) from Provence. Both freeze well and can be used in a variety of ways.

CAPONATA

	Olive oil	
3	medium eggplants, cubed	3
3	red or green bell peppers, cubed	3
2	onions, cut into large chunks	2
6 cups	coarsely chopped, peeled, seeded tomatoes (see Note below)	1.5 L
3	garlic cloves, minced	3
	Salt and pepper	
¼ cup	minced fresh basil	60 mL

Heat about 2 Tbsp. (30 mL) oil in a heavy skillet, and fry the eggplant for 4 to 5 minutes, stirring. Transfer to a large pot.

Add more oil to the skillet, and fry the peppers and onions for 4 to 5 minutes. Transfer to the pot, and add the tomatoes and garlic. Season with salt and pepper to taste, and cook over moderate heat, stirring frequently, until the sauce has thickened, 30 to 45 minutes depending on the water content of the tomatoes. Stir in the basil, and serve or freeze.

Serves 6-8

NOTE: Italian tomatoes are best, but any juicy red tomatoes will do, even canned stewed.

RATATOUILLE

Prepare Caponata as instructed, adding 3 zucchini, sliced, with the peppers and onions.

Here are a few suggestions for serving Caponata and Ratatouille:

- Serve cold as an hors d'oeuvre: Spoon the vegetable mixture into a lettuce leaf, like radicchio, or a phyllo pastry cup, then drizzle with olive oil and sprinkle with Parmesan cheese shavings (use a potato peeler to make shavings).
- Puree in a blender, adding a couple of tablespoons of olive oil for smoothness. Season with minced garlic and chopped fresh herbs, and serve as a dip with vegetables.
- Ladle over hot pasta, like a tomato sauce.
- Stuff crêpes, cover with grated mozzarella cheese; bake at 375°F (190°C) for 20 minutes.
- Use as a garnish for gougère.

FLAGEOLET AND ROOT SALAD

A tasty addition to a salad bar, this warm bean salad makes a filling lunch and is a perfect side dish for Leek and Chèvre Quiche (page 81). Canned beans can be substituted for cooked.

2	parsnips	2
1	small celery root	1
2 Tbsp.	olive oil	30 mL
¼ cup	white vermouth or white wine	60 mL
2 cups	cooked flageolets or white beans	500 mL
1 Tbsp.	dried herbs	15 mL
	Salt and pepper	

Peel the parsnips and celery root, and cut into 2-inch (5 cm) sticks ¼ inch (6 mm) thick.

Heat the oil in a large skillet, add the parsnips and celery root, and cook over medium heat until the vegetables are brown at the edges. Add the vermouth or wine, cover, and steam for a couple of minutes, until the vegetables are almost cooked.

Add the flageolets or beans and the herbs, season with salt and pepper to taste, and heat through.

Serves 4

VARIATION: Make a "meal in a bowl." Brush a boneless, skinless chicken breast with olive oil, and sprinkle liberally with dried herbs. Fry in a nonstick pan over medium-high heat for 5 minutes on each side, more if the meat is thick. Remove from heat, cover, and let stand for 5 minutes. Cut the chicken diagonally into strips. Toss with the warm bean salad.

ACORN POTPIE

A stunning look combined with a savory filling make these stuffed squash a favorite.

	PASTRY	
1½ cups	all-purpose flour	375 mL
½ tsp.	salt	2 mL
⅓ cup	vegetable shortening	75 mL
⅓ cup	cold butter	75 mL
3-4 Tbsp.	cold water	45-50 mL
4	acorn squash	4

	FILLING	
½ lb.	boneless chicken breast, cubed	250 g
	Olive oil	
	Dried herbs	
1 cup	quartered mushrooms	250 mL
3	carrots, diced	3
1 cup	chicken stock	250 mL
1 cup	green peas, fresh or frozen	250 mL
	Salt and pepper	
1 Tbsp.	all-purpose flour	15 mL
1 Tbsp.	butter	15 mL
1	egg, beaten	1

TO MAKE PASTRY: Combine the flour and salt. Cut in the shortening and butter until the mixture resembles breadcrumbs. Add the water 1 Tbsp. (15 mL) at a time until the dough forms a ball. Work the dough as little as possible. Wrap and chill for 1 hour.

Cut off the top of each squash (about 1 inch/2.5 cm thick), and scrape out the seeds and filaments inside. Brush the cut surfaces lightly with oil, and place, cut side down, on a cookie sheet. Bake at 375°F (190°C) for 20 minutes, until just tender. With a spoon, hollow out the centers, leaving a ½-inch (1 cm) shell. Set aside. (Reserve the pulp for another use.)

TO MAKE FILLING: While the squash are baking, marinate the chicken in a mixture of 2 Tbsp. (30 mL) oil and 1 Tbsp. (15 mL) herbs.

In a large nonstick skillet, heat 1 Tbsp. (15 mL) oil and stir-fry chicken over medium-high heat to seal, about 1 minute. Remove the chicken with a slotted spoon, and set aside.

Add more oil to the skillet, if necessary, and stir-fry the mushrooms until they are brown. Add the carrots and the stock, bring to a boil, then cover and simmer for 5 minutes. Add the chicken and the peas, and season with salt and pepper to taste.

Combine the flour and butter to form a paste (called beurre manié), and stir into the cooking liquid. Simmer until thickened, 1 to 2 minutes.

Roll out the dough ½ inch (1 cm) thick. Cut rounds of dough slightly larger than the squash tops. Spoon the filling into the squash. Cover with the dough rounds, and press the sides to seal. Decorate with dough trimmings, brush with egg, and bake in the preheated oven until the top is brown and crisp, about 20 minutes.

Serves 4

TIP: To make the squash stand upright, slice off the bottom tip or place in ramekin molds.

Thick Vegetable Pie, page 98

THICK VEGETABLE PIE

Okay! This recipe looks like a lot of work—and it is—but trust me, it's worth the effort.

PIE CRUST

3 cups	all-purpose flour	750 mL
½ tsp.	salt	2 mL
½ cup	vegetable shortening	125 mL
½ cup	cold butter	125 mL
1	egg	1
1 Tbsp.	white vinegar	15 mL
3-4 Tbsp.	cold water	45-60 mL

FILLING

	Olive oil	
2 cups	minced onions	500 mL
2 cups	sliced sunchokes	500 mL
1 cup	sliced celery root	250 mL
2 cups	cooked greens, such as spinach, kale or Swiss chard	500 mL
2 cups	grated mozzarella cheese	500 mL
2 cups	grated carrots or butternut squash	500 mL
	Salt and pepper	
3	eggs, plus 1 beaten egg	3
2 cups	white sauce (see page 66)	500 mL

TO MAKE PIE CRUST: Combine the flour and salt. Cut in the shortening and butter until the mixture resembles breadcrumbs. Add the egg and vinegar. Then add the water, 1 tablespoon (15 mL) at a time, until the dough holds together. Do not overwork. Wrap and chill the dough for 1 hour.

TO MAKE FILLING: Heat 2 Tbsp. (30 mL) oil in a pan, and cook the onions over medium heat until golden, about 5 minutes. Set aside.

Steam or microwave the sunchokes and the celery root, separately, until just tender. Set aside.

Set aside one-third of the dough for the top. Roll out the remaining dough, and line a greased 10-inch (3 L) springform pan, allowing 1 inch (2.5 cm) to hang over the sides.

Spread the onions in the bottom of the pan, and cover with the sunchokes. Continue the layering with the greens, mozzarella, carrots or squash and celery root, seasoning lightly with salt and pepper between each layer.

Beat the 3 eggs into the white sauce, and pour over the vegetables.

Roll out the reserved dough, cover the pan, trim the edges, and seal. Brush the top with beaten egg, and make a hole in the middle to allow the steam to escape. Bake at 375°F (190°C) for 1 hour, or until a toothpick inserted in the center comes out clean.

Let cool on a rack for 10 minutes before removing the sides of the pan.

Serves 8-10

STUFFED VEGETABLES

When I was growing up in France, my mother worked 48-hour weeks making cigars in a factory and still had time to prepare two meals a day. Workers had a two-hour lunch break. She would leave work at noon and stop at the butcher, the grocer and the baker on her way home, and by 12:35 p.m., she would have a delicious meal on the table. Only now do I realize what a daily tour de force that was.

From her, I learned to use few ingredients—but always the best—to minimize cooking steps and to make do with what I have on hand. I also learned how to prepare these stuffed vegetables, which I loved as a kid and still do.

You can stuff tomatoes, bell peppers, eggplants, zucchini (the round type called eightball are best), onions (choose round ones) and kohlrabi. Tomatoes do not need to be precooked.

4	medium eggplants	4
4	large onions	4
2	slices of white bread, crust removed	2
½ lb.	ground pork	250 g
½ lb.	ground veal	250 g
2	eggs	2
1 tsp.	salt	5 mL
1 tsp.	pepper	5 mL
1 tsp.	fresh or dried herbs	5 mL
	Breadcrumbs	

Cut each eggplant in half lengthwise, place in a microwave-safe dish with 2 Tbsp. (30 mL) water, and cook in the microwave oven for 3 minutes on high. Set aside. Peel the onions, and cut in half lengthwise. Cook as you did the eggplants, and set aside.

With a spoon, scoop out the centers of the eggplants, leaving a shell ½ inch (1 cm) thick. (Reserve the scooped-out eggplant for another use.) Scoop out the onions, leaving two outer layers, and reserve the insides. Set aside.

Soak the bread in cold water. When soft, drain and squeeze out most of the liquid.

Chop the reserved onion pulp, and combine with the pork, veal, eggs and bread. Add the salt, pepper and herbs, and mix well.

Fill the eggplant and onion shells with the meat mixture. Sprinkle the tops with breadcrumbs.

Place the stuffed vegetables in a greased shallow baking dish, and bake at 375°F (190°C) for 25 to 30 minutes, until the juices are clear.

Serves 4

VARIATION: For a vegetarian delight, combine the chopped onion pulp with 1 cup (250 mL) cooked millet or rice, ½ cup (125 mL) pitted and chopped black olives, 1 cup (250 mL) grated cheese and salt and pepper to taste. Fill the onion shells with the cheese mixture, and bake for 20 minutes.

STUFFED SQUASH

I use ambercup squash for this recipe, but you can also use pumpkin, kabocha, buttercup or any thick-skinned winter squash.

1	squash (about 5 lb./2.2 kg)	1
	Olive oil	
	Salt	
2	large onions, chopped	2
½ lb.	ground pork	250 g
½ cup	chopped fresh parsley	125 mL
½ cup	cooked greens (spinach, kale or Swiss chard)	125 mL
1	egg	1
½ cup	couscous, or more	125 mL
	Dried herbs	
	Pepper	
	Breadcrumbs	
	Grated Parmesan cheese	

Cut off the top of the squash, and set aside. Scrape out the seeds and filaments. Brush the inside with oil, sprinkle with salt, and set aside.

In a skillet, heat 2 Tbsp. (30 mL) oil and cook the onions until soft, about 2 minutes. Remove the onions with a slotted spoon, and set aside. In the same skillet, brown the pork, then stir in the onions, parsley, greens and egg.

Now try to judge how much couscous you need so that the stuffing will fill the squash.

Soak the couscous in an equal amount of warm water until soft. Drain and mix with the meat mixture and herbs, and season with salt and pepper to taste. Spoon the stuffing into the squash, cover with the squash lid, and bake at 400°F (200°C) for 1 hour 15 minutes.

Mix together an equal amount of breadcrumbs and cheese. Remove the squash lid, and sprinkle the top with the breadcrumb mixture. Place under the broiler until the top is crisp.

To serve, cut the squash into equal portions or scoop out the stuffing and squash and place in a serving bowl.

Serves 4-6

MOSTLY MEAT

Lamb Shanks With Onion and Apple Compote;
Grilled Root Vegetables, page 124

ROAST CHICKEN
WITH HERB AND CHEESE STUFFING

Spreading cheese and herbs under the skin of the chicken will prevent the meat from becoming dry, and flattening the chicken will ensure even cooking. Choose a fresh chicken with a thick, healthy skin.

1	3 lb. (1.5 kg) roasting chicken	1
1 cup	feta or goat cheese	250 mL
1 cup	sour cream or creamy cottage cheese	250 mL
3 Tbsp.	chopped fresh herbs (rosemary, basil, marjoram), or 1 Tbsp. (15 mL) dried	45 mL
	Olive oil	
1	onion, thinly sliced	1
10	garlic cloves	10
½ cup	white wine	125 mL
	Salt and pepper	

With kitchen scissors or a sharp knife, cut the chicken along each side of the spine, remove the spine, turn the chicken over, and flatten with the palms of your hands. Pinch the skin all over, then carefully lift and work the skin away from the meat.

Combine the cheese, sour cream or cottage cheese, herbs and 2 Tbsp. (30 mL) oil. Mix well. Spread this mixture between the meat and the skin, smoothing as you go.

In a large baking dish, make a bed of onion slices and garlic cloves, add the wine, and set the chicken on top. Brush the chicken with oil, and season with salt and pepper to taste. Roast at 400°F (200°C) for 30 minutes, then lower the oven temperature to 375°F (190°C), and cook for 1 hour, basting several times, until the juices run clear.

Serve with Tian (page 89) or with a medley of spring vegetables (page 85) and grilled polenta (page 71).

Serves 4

CHICKEN CACCIATORE

Chicken skin may be delicious when roasted, but it doesn't look too appetizing when stewed, so I prefer to remove it. However, if the skin is removed before cooking, the meat tends to fall apart. If you want to have presentable chicken pieces, remove the skin after stewing. This dish freezes well.

2	3 lb. (1.5 kg) roasting chickens, or the equivalent weight in chicken legs	2
⅓ cup	olive oil	75 mL
4	onions, minced	4
6 cups	peeled and coarsely chopped tomatoes	1.5 L
4 cups	quartered mushrooms	1 L
	Salt and pepper	
¼ cup	chopped fresh herbs (rosemary, marjoram, basil)	60 mL

If using whole chickens, cut them into individual pieces.

In a large, heavy pot, heat the oil and cook the onions over medium heat until soft. Remove with a slotted spoon, and set aside. In the same pot, fry the chicken pieces until browned on all sides. Add the onions, tomatoes and mushrooms. Season with salt and pepper to taste. Cover and simmer for 45 minutes (15 minutes in a pressure cooker), or until the chicken is tender. Stir in the herbs.

Before serving, remove the skin from the chicken pieces, if desired.

Serves 6

CHICKEN WITH APPLE CIDER

Like all braised dishes, this one tastes even better the next day, when the flavors have had a chance to spend more time together.

	Olive oil	
4	chicken thighs	4
16	small onions, peeled	16
4	large cooking apples, peeled and quartered	4
1½ cups	dry apple cider	375 mL
	Salt and pepper	

Heat 2 Tbsp. (30 mL) oil in a skillet, and brown the chicken on all sides over high heat. Transfer to a baking dish.

Add more oil to the skillet, if necessary, and cook the onions over medium heat until they are slightly colored, then add to the chicken. In the same skillet, cook the apples for 2 minutes. Add to the chicken and onions.

Deglaze the skillet with the cider, and pour it over the chicken. Season with salt and pepper to taste. Cover and bake at 375°F (190°C) for 45 minutes, or until the chicken is cooked.

Ladle most of the sauce into a small saucepan, and reduce over high heat until thick. Pour the sauce over the chicken, and serve with fresh pasta or creamy mashed potatoes.

Serves 4

LOVAGE POT-AU-FEU

If using a pressure cooker, you can prepare this complete meal for four to six people in 20 minutes. To save another 5 minutes in preparation time, do not stuff the chicken. You can also use other types of root vegetables, such as sweet potatoes, celery root or parsnips.

STUFFING

2 cups	chopped fresh spinach or kale	500 mL
½ cup	uncooked rice	125 mL
1	egg	1
2 tsp.	salt	10 mL
1 Tbsp.	mixed dried herbs	15 mL
1	3 lb. (1.5 kg) roasting chicken	1
2 cups	water	500 mL
4	small turnips, peeled	4
4	carrots, peeled and cut into chunks	4
2	potatoes, peeled and quartered	2
2	lovage sprigs	2
1	bay leaf	1
	Salt and pepper	

TO MAKE STUFFING: Combine the spinach or kale, rice, egg, salt and herbs. Loosely stuff the chicken; do not pack tightly, as the rice will expand during cooking.

Place the chicken in a pressure cooker, add the water, vegetables, lovage, bay leaf and salt and pepper to taste, and cook for 15 minutes. (Always remember to start timing when

the air vent whistles or turns.) Or put the chicken in a large, heavy pot, and cover with water. Bring slowly to a boil, then simmer until the chicken is cooked, 45 minutes to 1 hour. Add the vegetables and seasonings halfway through the cooking time so that they do not overcook.

For the first course, serve the bouillon with croutons and grated Parmesan cheese, then bring the chicken and vegetables to the table with a choice of sauces (see pages 114 and 115), mustards and herb-flavored mayonnaise.

Serves 6-8

ROMESCO SAUCE

I discovered this sauce in Spain, where it is served with roasted baby leeks. If you "like it hot," increase the number of hot peppers.

1	garlic head	1
½ cup	olive oil	125 mL
4	red bell peppers	4
1	hot pepper, or more to taste	1
	Salt and pepper	

Peel the garlic cloves, and place in a small baking dish. Pour the oil over the garlic, and cover with aluminum foil. Place the whole red peppers and the hot pepper in another baking dish. Bake the garlic and the peppers at 375°F (190°C) for about 45 minutes, turning the peppers until they are roasted on all sides.

Remove the skin and seeds from the peppers, and place the peppers in the bowl of a food processor or blender. Remove the garlic cloves from the oil with a slotted spoon, and add to the peppers. (Reserve the garlic oil for another use; it is a flavorful addition to salad dressings.) Cream at high speed. Season with salt and pepper to taste.

Makes about 1½ cups (375 mL)

SAUCE GRIBICHE

1	hard-boiled egg	1
1 Tbsp.	tarragon vinegar or lemon juice	15 mL
1 Tbsp.	Dijon mustard	15 mL
1 cup	olive oil	250 mL
2 Tbsp.	chopped fresh parsley	30 mL
1 Tbsp.	chopped capers	15 mL
	Salt and pepper	

Mash the egg yolk with a fork, and mix with the vinegar or lemon juice and the mustard. Whisk in the oil in a slow, steady stream until the sauce is thick and creamy.

Add the parsley, capers and egg white, finely chopped. Season with salt and pepper to taste.

Kale

I can never grow enough kale. The tender young leaves are delicious raw, and the large leaves freeze well. I pick the leaves all summer long for fresh eating and freeze at least three big harvests. It can be used in soups, fillings (phyllo rolls) and stuffing for poultry (Lovage Pot-au-Feu, page 112) and can also be served as a side dish. Like all members of the cabbage family, kale is a healthful, versatile green that is good for you; it is particularly recommended for the prevention of cancer.

TO FREEZE KALE: Wash and drain leaves, but do not shake off water. Place leaves, whole or coarsely chopped, in a nonstick pan. Cover and cook (without oil or butter) over medium-high heat until the leaves are wilted. Drain in a colander, and let cool. Press leaves between the palms of your hands to remove excess water; freeze in plastic freezer bags.

PORK TENDERLOIN STUFFED WITH APPLES

This comfort food is also refined and elegant—a winning combination.

½ cup	hazelnuts, skin removed	125 mL
2	apples, peeled and coarsely grated	2
	Pinch each of ground cinnamon and allspice	
2	pork loins (about ¾ lb./375 g each)	2
2 Tbsp.	unsalted butter	30 mL
1 Tbsp.	all-purpose flour	15 mL
1½ cups	apple juice	375 mL
	Salt and pepper	

Coarsely chop the hazelnuts, and mix with the apples, cinnamon and allspice.

Cut the pork loins in half lengthwise, being careful not to cut all the way through. Stuff each loin with one-half of the apple mixture, and tie with kitchen string.

Melt the butter in a skillet, and brown the loins on all sides. Transfer the loins to a baking dish. Sprinkle the flour in the skillet, and cook for a few seconds, then add the apple juice and stir, scraping with a wooden spoon. Pour the liquid over the pork loins. Cover and bake at 375°F (190°C) for 45 minutes.

Transfer the pork to a serving dish, and keep warm. Reduce the sauce over high heat until thickened, about 15 minutes, and season with salt and pepper to taste.

Cut the pork into thick slices, spoon the sauce over, and serve with creamy mashed potatoes or rice.

Serves 4

CHARLOTTE WITH APPLES AND PORK

The original charlotte is an 18th-century English dessert made with fruit and baked in a bread-lined mold. There are also savory charlottes, like this one, and cold desserts, such as charlotte russe, created by the celebrated French chef Antonin Carême for the Russian Czar Aleksandr I.

10	slices white or brown bread	10
	Butter	
½ lb.	ground pork	250 g
½ lb.	chicken livers	250 g
4	apples, peeled and grated	4
1 cup	chopped fresh parsley	250 mL
1	egg	1
½ Tbsp.	salt	8 mL
½ tsp.	pepper	2 mL
	RED WINE SAUCE	
¼ cup	plus 1 Tbsp. (15 mL) butter	60 mL
1	onion, minced	1
1 cup	red wine	250 mL
2 cups	beef stock	500 mL
	Salt and pepper	
	Chopped fresh herbs	
1 Tbsp.	all-purpose flour	15 mL

Remove the bread crusts, and butter one side of each bread slice. Place the slices on a baking sheet, butter side up, and broil until golden. Let cool.

Preheat the oven to 375°F (190°C).

In the bowl of a food processor, combine the pork, chicken livers, apples, parsley, egg, salt and pepper, and process at high speed until well mixed. Or chop the livers by hand, and mix with the remaining ingredients in a large bowl. Grease a charlotte or soufflé mold, and line the bottom and sides with the bread, arranging the slices so that the toasted side faces outward. Spoon in the apple-and-pork mixture, and cover tightly with aluminum foil.

Put the mold in a pan with 1 inch (2.5 cm) of hot water, and place on the center rack of the preheated oven. Immediately lower the oven temperature to 350°F (180°C), and bake for 1½ to 2 hours, until the juices run clear. Let the charlotte cool in the mold for 15 minutes.

Meanwhile, make the red wine sauce. In a heavy saucepan, melt ¼ cup (60 mL) butter, and cook the onion over medium heat until soft, about 2 minutes. Add the wine, and bring to a boil. Cook for 1 minute to evaporate the alcohol. Add the stock, and cook over high heat until the liquid is reduced by half. Season with salt and pepper to taste, and add herbs to taste (tarragon is great, and so is rosemary).

In a small bowl, combine 1 Tbsp. (15 mL) butter and the flour until it forms a soft paste. Whisk into the wine mixture, and cook over medium heat until the sauce has thickened. Do not boil.

Unmold the charlotte on a serving dish, and pass the sauce at the table.

Serves 4-6

FARCIS ORLÉANAIS (Stuffed Lettuce, Orléans-Style)

I like to use a blend of pork and veal for any type of stuffing. The bread and eggs help hold the bundles together and keep them moist.

3	slices white bread	3
2	large heads of Boston lettuce	2
½ lb.	ground pork	250 g
⅓ lb.	ground veal	150 g
2	eggs	2
1½ tsp.	salt	7 mL
1 tsp.	dried oregano	5 mL
4	slices bacon	4
2	carrots, peeled and thinly sliced	2
2	onions, minced	2
1	bay leaf	1
½ cup	chicken stock	125 mL

Remove the bread crusts, and soak the slices in water until soft. Drain, then press between the palms of your hands to remove excess liquid. Set aside.

Sprinkle the lettuce heads with 2 Tbsp. (30 mL) water, and steam on the stovetop or cook in the microwave oven on high for 2 minutes, until wilted. Drain, and let cool slightly.

Set aside 16 large lettuce leaves. Chop the remaining lettuce, and combine it with the bread, pork, veal, eggs, salt and oregano. Mix well.

Spread out four lettuce leaves so that they are overlapping, place one-quarter of the meat filling in the middle, fold over, and secure the bundle with a bacon strip. Repeat with the remaining 12 lettuce leaves to make a total of four bundles.

Spread the carrots and onions in the bottom of a baking dish, add the bay leaf, and place the bundles on top. Add the stock, cover and bake at 300°F (150°C) for 1 hour.

Serves 4

LAMB SHANKS WITH ONION
AND APPLE COMPOTE

The best-tasting parts of the lamb are the shanks and the shoulder.

	Olive oil	
4	large onions, minced	4
4	lamb shanks (about ¾ lb./375 g each)	4
	Salt and pepper	
1 cup	apple juice	250 mL
1	apple, peeled and grated	1
2	sprigs fresh rosemary	2

	GRILLED ROOT VEGETABLES	
2	parsnips	2
2	carrots	2
1	sweet potato or small turnip	1
¼ cup	olive oil	60 mL
	Salt and pepper	
2 Tbsp.	balsamic vinegar	30 mL

In a large skillet, heat ¼ cup (60 mL) oil, and cook the onions over medium heat until soft and just turning golden, about 3 minutes. Remove the onions from the skillet with a slotted spoon, and spread in the bottom of a large baking dish.

Add a little oil to the skillet, if necessary, and fry the shanks until browned on all sides. Arrange the shanks on top of the onions. Season with salt and pepper to taste. Add the apple juice, cover and bake at 375°F (190°C) for 1 hour.

Stir in the apple and rosemary, lower the oven temperature to 350°F (180°C), and bake for 30 minutes, until the shanks are tender.

Meanwhile, peel and cut the vegetables into julienne sticks 2 inches (5 cm) long and ¼ inch (6 mm) thick. Blanch the vegetables in boiling water for 2 minutes, then drain and pat dry. Or cook the vegetables in the microwave oven on high for 2 minutes.

Heat the oil in a heavy skillet, and cook the vegetables over medium heat until they are browned, adding more oil, if necessary. Season with salt and pepper to taste, and drizzle with vinegar.

Serve the lamb shanks with the vegetables and grilled polenta (page 71).

Serves 4

LAMB STEW, MOROCCAN-STYLE

This Moroccan stew can also be made with prunes and cooked in a traditional earthenware dish called tajine.

1 tsp.	each of cumin seeds, caraway seeds, coriander seeds, black peppercorns	5 mL
1 Tbsp.	unsalted butter	15 mL
1 Tbsp.	olive oil	15 mL
2 lb.	lamb shoulder, cubed	1 kg
	All-purpose flour	
12	dried apricots	12
6	dried figs	6
1	star anise (optional)	1
1½ cups	water	375 mL
	Salt and pepper	
	Pinch of saffron or turmeric (optional)	

Reduce the seeds and peppercorns to a powder with a spice grinder or a mortar and pestle.

In a large nonstick skillet, heat the butter and the oil together. Add the ground spices, and cook for 30 seconds, stirring constantly.

Coat the lamb with flour, shake off excess, and brown on all sides in the spiced oil over medium heat. Transfer to a baking dish with a lid.

Insert the apricots and figs among the meat pieces, and add the star anise, if using.

Add the water and 2 tsp. (10 mL) salt to the skillet, swirl to gather all meat particles and spices, then pour over the lamb. Cover and bake at 325°F (160°C) for 60 to 75 minutes.

Transfer the lamb and the fruits to a serving dish. Keep warm.

Reduce the sauce over high heat until thick, and season with salt and pepper to taste. If desired, add saffron or turmeric to brighten the color. Pour the sauce over the lamb.

Serve with jasmine rice.

Serves 6-8

BEEF PROVENÇALE

Don't forget the orange peel—it makes a real difference. This stew is perfect for freezing.

2	onions, minced	2
	Bouquet garni	
	Grated peel of 1 orange	
3 lb.	stewing beef, cut into cubes	1.5 kg
2 cups	white wine	500 mL
	Olive oil	
2	carrots, peeled and thickly sliced	2
2 cups	quartered mushrooms	500 mL
4	tomatoes, peeled and coarsely chopped	4
1 cup	pitted black olives	250 mL
	Salt and pepper	

Place the onions, bouquet garni, orange peel and beef in a large nonmetallic baking dish, pour the wine over, and drizzle with a little oil. Cover and marinate overnight in the refrigerator.

Arrange the carrots, mushrooms, tomatoes and olives on top of the meat, season with salt and pepper to taste, cover and bake at 350°F (180°C) for 2 hours.

Serve with fresh pasta tossed with olive oil and grated Parmesan cheese.

Serves 6

RABBIT VOL-AU-VENT

This recipe works just as well with chicken.

3	rabbit legs, or 1 saddle	3
	(about 1 lb./500 g)	
	Olive oil	
	Fresh or dried mixed herbs	
1	onion, minced	1
1	celery stalk, chopped	1
1 cup	white wine	250 mL
1 cup	water	250 mL
2 cups	quartered mushrooms	500 mL
	Salt and pepper	
2 Tbsp.	butter	30 mL
1 Tbsp.	all-purpose flour	15 mL
4	puff pastry shells	4

Remove the bones from the rabbit, and cut the meat into bite-sized pieces. Toss with 1 Tbsp. (15 mL) oil and a pinch of herbs. Marinate for 1 hour.

In a heavy skillet, heat 2 Tbsp. (30 mL) oil, and cook the onion for 1 minute, until soft. Add the celery, wine and water. Bring to a boil, and cook over high heat until the liquid is reduced by half. Transfer the mixture to a bowl, and set aside.

Add 2 Tbsp. (30 mL) oil to the skillet, and cook the mushrooms over high heat until golden. Remove the mushrooms with a slotted spoon, and set aside.

Add more oil to the skillet, and cook the marinated meat for 2 minutes, until browned on all sides. Add the onion-celery mixture and the mushrooms. Season with salt and pepper and herbs to taste. Cover and simmer for 20 minutes, until the meat is cooked.

Mix the butter with the flour until it forms a soft paste. Add to the meat mixture, and stir until the sauce has thickened.

Warm the puff pastry shells (or cook if frozen). Divide the meat mixture among the shells, spooning the sauce over all, and serve with greens and a carrot or turnip puree.

Serves 4

BREADS

Oatmeal Rolls, page 140

BASIC PIZZA DOUGH

For extra flavor, add a couple of tablespoons of dried oregano, marjoram, basil and/or rosemary to the flour (double the quantity if using fresh herbs).

2 Tbsp.	active dry yeast	30 mL
1 tsp.	sugar	5 mL
1½ cups	lukewarm water, or more	375 mL
6-7 cups	all-purpose flour	1.5-1.75 L
½ cup	olive oil	125 mL
1 Tbsp.	salt	15 mL

Dissolve the yeast and sugar in 1 cup (250 mL) of the water. Let stand until bubbly.

Combine 2 cups (500 mL) of the flour with the oil and the salt. Add the yeast mixture, and blend well. Add the remaining flour, 1 cup (250 mL) at a time, and enough of the remaining water to make a smooth, elastic dough. Turn out onto a floured surface, and knead for 5 minutes. If using a food processor, knead with the plastic blades for 3 minutes.

Place the dough in a lightly greased bowl, turning to grease all over. Cover, and let the dough rise in a warm place for 1 hour, or until double in size. (Note: If you place the bowl in a cooler with a pan of hot water and cover it, the dough will rise quickly and evenly.) Punch down. The dough is now ready to use.

I usually use half of the dough to make an extra-large pizza. While the oven is preheating, I roll out the dough for the pizza, garnish it and set it aside, then I prepare herb rolls or cheese sticks with the remaining dough. The rolls have time to rise when the pizza is in the oven, and they are baked while we eat the pizza.

Makes 3 large pizzas, 3 focaccias, 2 olive breads or 16 dinner rolls

Focaccia With Tomato Pesto, page 136;
Ham and Onion Log, page 137

FOCACCIA WITH TOMATO PESTO

½	Basic Pizza Dough (page 134)	½
½ cup	Tomato-Basil Paste (page 30)	125 mL
2 Tbsp.	olive oil	30 mL
1 Tbsp.	dried herbs	15 mL
	Rock salt	

Spread the dough with your fingers to make a 12-by-20-inch (30 x 50 cm) rectangle. Spread with half of the tomato pesto, fold, and spread with the remaining pesto. Drizzle the top with the oil, and sprinkle with the herbs and salt to taste. Let rise for 30 minutes.

Bake at 400°F (200°C) for 5 minutes, then lower the oven temperature to 375°F (190°C), and bake for 25 minutes.

Serves 4-6

TIP: Spray a little water in the oven at the beginning of baking. The steam will help the dough rise.

HAM AND ONION LOG

1	onion, minced	1
2 Tbsp.	olive oil	30 mL
1 cup	diced ham	250 mL
½	Basic Pizza Dough (page 134)	½

Cook the onion in the oil over medium-high heat for 2 minutes, add the ham, and cook, stirring, for 5 minutes. Remove from the heat, and set aside.

Roll out the dough to a 1-inch-thick (2.5 cm) rectangle, or spread the dough with the tips of your fingers. Spread the ham and onion over the dough. Starting with the longer side of the rectangle, roll the dough into a log shape. Place the log, seam side down, on a baking sheet, and let rise for 30 minutes.

Bake at 400°F (200°C) for 5 minutes, then lower the oven temperature to 375°F (190°C), and bake for 25 minutes.

Serves 4-6

VARIATIONS

❧ Add grated cheese, such as mozzarella, to the filling.

❧ For a vegetarian roll, replace the ham with sliced mushrooms.

❧ Cut the log into six portions, and bake the buns on a greased baking sheet.

PISSALADIÈRE

This traditional French dish with savory toppings was once sold by the slice on street corners.

1 cup	olive oil	250 mL
10	large onions, minced	10
	Salt and pepper	
½	Basic Pizza Dough (page 134)	½
12	black olives, or more to taste	12
6	anchovies (optional)	6
	Dried or fresh herbs (thyme, rosemary, marjoram)	

In a large, heavy saucepan, heat the oil and cook the onions over medium heat, stirring often, until they are soft and golden, about 20 minutes. Season with salt and pepper to taste (see Note below). Remove from the heat and set aside.

Preheat the oven to 400°F (200°C).

Roll out the dough or spread with your fingertips to a ½-inch-thick (1 cm) rectangle. Spread the onions on top, garnish with the olives and anchovies, if using, and sprinkle with herbs to taste.

Bake for 5 minutes, then lower the oven temperature to 375°F (190°C), and bake for 25 minutes.

Serves 4-6

NOTE: Onions become very sweet when they are cooked. Keep that in mind when you add salt. You may need more than you think.

OATMEAL ROLLS

Soft and with a hint of sweetness, these rolls are the perfect companion for cheese as well as jam.

2 cups	boiling water	500 mL
1 cup	quick-cooking rolled oats	250 mL
¼ cup	molasses or maple syrup	60 mL
2 Tbsp.	unsalted butter	30 mL
1½ tsp.	salt	7 mL
1 tsp.	sugar	5 mL
¼ cup	lukewarm water	60 mL
1 Tbsp.	active dry yeast	15 mL
2 cups	all-purpose flour, or more	500 mL
2 cups	whole wheat flour, or more	500 mL

In a large bowl, stir together the boiling water, rolled oats, molasses or maple syrup, butter and salt. Let the mixture cool.

Dissolve the sugar in the lukewarm water, sprinkle with the yeast, and let the mixture stand for 10 minutes, or until frothy. Stir into the oat mixture. Stir in half of the all-purpose flour and half of the whole wheat flour. Beat until smooth, about 3 minutes.

Gradually add the remaining flour, stirring with a wooden spoon. Knead the dough on a lightly floured surface until it is smooth and elastic, 5 to 8 minutes, adding more flour, as needed, if the dough is sticky. Place the dough in a lightly greased bowl, turning to grease all over. Cover the bowl, and let the dough rise in a warm place for 1 hour, or until double in size.

Punch down the dough, turn out onto a lightly floured surface, and form into a 12-inch-long (30 cm) log. Cut the dough into 12 pieces, and shape each piece into a ball. Place on a greased baking sheet, and let the dough rise for 30 minutes.

Bake at 375°F (190°C) for 20 to 25 minutes, until the bottom makes a hollow sound when tapped. Let the rolls cool on a rack.

Makes 12 rolls

BUTTERMILK FANS

There is definitely something "grandmotherly" about these light, silky pull-apart buns.

2 cups	warm buttermilk	500 mL
1 Tbsp.	active dry yeast	15 mL
4 cups	all-purpose flour	1 L
2 tsp.	salt	10 mL
¼ cup	sugar	60 mL
	Olive oil	
	Dried herbs (oregano, basil parsley)	

In a small bowl, combine 1 cup (250 mL) of the buttermilk and the yeast. Let the mixture stand in a warm place for 10 minutes, or until frothy.

In a large bowl, mix together 1 cup (250 mL) of the flour, the salt and the sugar. Beat in the yeast mixture and the remaining 1 cup (250 mL) buttermilk. Mix well. Add the remaining 3 cups (750 mL) flour, ½ cup (125 mL) at a time, beating with a wooden spoon. Knead the dough on a lightly floured surface for a couple of minutes. Place the dough in a greased bowl, cover and let rise in a warm place for 1 hour.

Gently punch down the dough, knead for 1 minute, then divide the dough in half.

Roll out half of the dough into a ⅓-inch-thick (8 mm) rectangle. Brush with oil, and sprinkle with herbs. Cut the dough lengthwise into four strips, and stack one on top of the other. Cut lengthwise again, and stack so that you have eight layers. Cut into 2-inch-wide (5 cm) pieces, and place sideways in buttered muffin tins. Repeat with the second batch of dough.

Let the dough rise until almost double in size, brush the tops with oil, and bake at 400°F (200°C) for 15 to 20 minutes, or until lightly browned.

Makes 16 buns

VARIATIONS

◦ Spread Tomato-Basil Paste (page 30) between the layers of dough, or sprinkle with grated Parmesan cheese.

◦ For sweet buns, use only ½ tsp. (2 mL) salt and increase the sugar to ½ cup (125 mL), then spread your favorite jam or jelly between the layers.

BRIOCHE

I love this sweet egg bread, so I always bake a big batch and freeze some. It also keeps fresh for quite a while in the refrigerator if stored in a paper bag inserted in a plastic one.

1 tsp.	sugar	5 mL
½ cup	lukewarm water	125 mL
2 Tbsp.	active dry yeast	30 mL
1 cup	warm buttermilk	250 mL
⅔ cup	melted unsalted butter	150 mL
1 Tbsp.	vanilla extract	15 mL
3	eggs	3
5 cups	all-purpose flour	1.25 L
1 cup	sugar	250 mL
1 tsp.	salt	5 mL
1 cup	seedless raisins	250 mL
½ cup	candied orange peel	125 mL

Dissolve 1 tsp. (5 mL) sugar in the water, stir in the yeast, and let stand in a warm place for 10 minutes, or until frothy.

Combine the buttermilk, butter, vanilla and 2 of the eggs, beaten. Stir into yeast mixture.

In a large bowl, combine 1 cup (250 mL) of the flour with 1 cup (250 mL) sugar and the salt. Whisk in the buttermilk mixture, and beat for 1 minute. With a wooden spoon, stir in the remaining 4 cups (1 L) flour, ½ cup (125 mL) at a time. When the dough begins to come away from the sides of the bowl, turn it out onto a lightly floured surface. Knead for about 10 minutes, until the dough is smooth and elastic. If using a food processor, knead for only 3 to 5 minutes.

Add the raisins and orange peel. Fold the dough several times until well combined.

Place the dough in a lightly greased bowl, cover and let rise in a warm place for about 1 hour, or until double in size.

Use butter to grease 1 large tube cake pan, 2 brioche molds or 3 bread molds. Punch the dough down gently, cut and place in the prepared pan(s). Or divide the dough into three balls, roll into long strips, braid it and place on a buttered baking sheet.

Allow the dough to rise for 30 to 45 minutes, or until almost double in size. Brush the top with the remaining egg, beaten, and bake at 350°F (180°C) for 25 to 35 minutes, until the bottom sounds hollow when tapped. Turn it out onto a rack, and let cool.

Serves 8-10

DESSERTS

Parsnip Pie, page 173

SWEET SCENTED CUSTARD

I flavor this delectable easy-to-make custard with leaves of scented geranium or lemon verbena. You can also use fresh mint leaves, lemon basil or vanilla extract. Always add a pinch of salt, even to sweet preparations, to pep up the flavors.

2 cups	milk	500 mL
½ cup	loosely packed scented geranium or lemon verbena leaves	125 mL
2	eggs	2
½ cup	sugar	125 mL
1 Tbsp.	cornstarch	15 mL
	Pinch of salt	
1 Tbsp.	unsalted butter	15 mL

In a heavy saucepan, heat the milk with the scented leaves, and simmer for 10 minutes. Strain the milk, and discard the leaves.

In a bowl, beat together the eggs, sugar, cornstarch and salt. Add about ½ cup (125 mL) of the flavored milk, stir, and return to the pan with the remaining flavored milk. Cook over medium heat, stirring constantly with a wooden spoon, until thickened, about 5 minutes. Stir in the butter until melted.

Spoon the custard over Apple Bread Pudding (page 157), or use to make Berries au Gratin (page 151).

Makes 2 cups (500 mL)

BERRIES AU GRATIN

I like to make this dessert with frozen raspberries. Because the cooking time is so short, the berries do not thaw completely and are a fantastic combination with the warm custard. Allow one cup (250 mL) of berries per serving.

Fresh or frozen berries
(raspberries, blueberries, blackberries)
Sweet Scented Custard (page 148)
Sugar

Spread the berries in individual shallow baking dishes (I use ramekins), cover with custard, and sprinkle with sugar. Broil until the tops are caramelized, about 5 minutes.

Freezing berries

To freeze whole berries, simply spread the berries on a baking sheet and place in the freezer. When they are frozen, store in the freezer in a rigid container or a freezer bag.

Raspberries and blueberries freeze beautifully—they retain their shape, color and flavor very well—while whole strawberries turn mushy and gray when thawed.

To freeze strawberries, slice them and place alternate layers of berries and a sprinkling of sugar in a rigid container, then freeze; use for pies. Or puree the fresh strawberries in a blender, add sugar to taste, and freeze in a small, rigid container; use to make coulis.

CHOCOLATE AND RASPBERRY CLAFOUTIS

An old-fashioned French dessert, clafoutis is traditionally made with Bing cherries. I prefer to make it with raspberries (I have lots of them), but you can also use large blueberries.

	Sugar	
	Fresh raspberries (enough to cover	
	the bottom of the baking pan;	
	about 3 cups/750 mL)	
½ cup	all-purpose flour	125 mL
1 tsp.	baking powder	5 mL
1 tsp.	baking soda	5 mL
¼ cup	powdered cocoa	60 mL
	Pinch of salt	
2	eggs, separated	2
¼ cup	butter	60 mL
½ cup	sugar	125 mL
2	squares semisweet chocolate	2
¼ cup	buttermilk or light cream	60 mL

Butter a 9-by-12-inch (3 L) square baking dish, sprinkle the bottom with sugar, and spread the fruit in the dish.

Combine the dry ingredients, and set aside. Beat together the egg yolks, butter and

sugar until creamy and light in color. Melt the chocolate in the microwave or in a small saucepan over low heat, and add to the egg-yolk mixture. Beat in the dry ingredients, alternating with the buttermilk or cream.

Beat the egg whites until stiff, and fold into the batter. Spoon the batter over the fruit, level the top with a spatula, and bake at 375°F (190°C) for 40 to 45 minutes, or until it is firm in the middle.

Serve warm or cold with heavy cream or Sweet Scented Custard (page 148).

Serves 6-8

BAKED APPLES IN WINE

These apples warm up beautifully the next day in the microwave oven and, in fact, are even tastier.

Cooking apples (6-10)

Cold unsalted butter

Chopped mixed nuts

(blanched almonds, cashews, pecans)

Brown sugar

Ground cinnamon

1 cup	red wine	250 mL
½ cup	water	125 mL

Use as many apples as your baking dish will hold. Wash and core the apples, and place in a baking dish. Push a small piece of butter (about the size of a cherry) into the bottom of each hole, fill with nuts, top with 1 tsp. (5 mL) brown sugar, and sprinkle with cinnamon. Pour the wine and water into the dish, and bake at 375°F (190°C) for 30 minutes.

Serve with Sweet Scented Custard (page 148).

APPLE BREAD PUDDING

Here is a great way to use up stale or leftover bread—whole wheat or multigrain, white bread, egg bread, even raisin bread. It can be served warm or cold.

1 cup	sugar	250 mL
2 Tbsp.	water	30 mL
1 Tbsp.	lemon juice	15 mL
3	eggs	3
2 cups	warm milk	500 mL
4 cups	cubed whole wheat bread (about 6 slices)	1 L
2	apples, peeled and diced	2
1 tsp.	vanilla extract	5 mL
½ cup	maple syrup or sugar	125 mL

In a heavy saucepan, heat the sugar with the water and lemon juice over medium-high heat until the mixture forms a golden syrup, 8 to 10 minutes. Do not stir. Pour the caramel sauce into a baking dish, and swirl to coat the bottom and sides. Set aside.

Alternatively, the caramel sauce can be prepared in a microwave oven in a deep 4-cup (1 L) glass or ceramic baking dish. Combine the sugar, water and lemon juice in the baking dish. Microwave on high for 5 to 7 minutes, until the sauce is a rich caramel color.

In a large bowl, beat the eggs, then add the milk and the bread cubes. Let stand for 5 minutes to soften the bread. Stir in the apples, vanilla extract and maple syrup or sugar.

Pour the mixture into the baking dish, and bake at 375°F (190°C) for 35 minutes. Let cool on a rack; unmold and spoon Sweet Scented Custard (page 148) over each serving.

Serves 4-6

QUICK APPLE PIE

As this pie is best served warm, prepare the pie shell and cook the apples earlier in the day, and keep refrigerated until you are ready for dessert. After the main course, while your guests are relaxing or eating fine cheeses, assemble and bake the pie.

3	phyllo pastry sheets	3
½ cup	butter, melted	125 mL
¼ cup	sugar	60 mL
¼ cup	ground almonds or hazelnuts	60 mL

FILLING

2 Tbsp.	unsalted butter	30 mL
4	cooking apples, peeled and cubed	4
¼ cup	brown sugar	60 mL
¼ cup	toasted slivered almonds	60 mL

Spread 1 sheet of phyllo pastry in a pie plate, brush with the butter, and sprinkle with half of the sugar and ground nuts. Spread another sheet of pastry over the first; brush with butter and sprinkle with the remaining sugar and ground nuts. Place the third sheet on top, letting the excess pastry extend over the edge of the pie plate.

To make the filling, melt the butter in a skillet, and cook the apples over medium heat until just soft. Transfer the apples to the pie shell. Sprinkle with the brown sugar and toasted almonds, and fold the excess pastry over the filling. Bake at 375°F (190°C) for 15 minutes, until golden. Serve warm.

Serves 4

QUICK APPLE TART

I was once invited to a gourmet weekend at a hunting lodge way up north, where a chef from Lyon, France, dazzled us with his talent. A charming man, he let me hang around the kitchen while he prepared sautéed foie gras, pike quenelles and this apple tart. I was impressed by the simplicity of such a spectacular dessert, which proves what I have always maintained: Gourmet cuisine doesn't need to be complicated. I was, however, appalled by the amount of sugar he sprinkled over the apples. I cut the amount by half and am quite happy with the results.

1	package (396 g) frozen puff pastry	1
8	cooking apples	8
¼ cup	unsalted butter	60 mL
1 cup	sugar	250 mL
	Confectioners' sugar (optional)	

Roll out each block of dough to a 12-inch (30 cm) square (you may also roll it into a circle to make two tarts). Peel and core the apples, and cut into thin slices. Arrange the slices on the pastry. Dot the apples with the butter, and sprinkle with 1 cup (250 mL) sugar. Bake at 350°F (180°C) for 30 minutes. Place under the broiler for a few minutes to caramelize the top.

Serve warm or cold, sprinkled with confectioners' sugar, if desired.

Serves 6-8

GÂTEAU RUSTIQUE

When wild apples are plentiful, I prepare several batches of this moist, tender cake. I cut each cake into four to six portions, wrap the pieces individually in plastic wrap, and freeze.

2 cups	all-purpose flour	500 mL
4 tsp.	baking powder	20 mL
½ Tbsp.	baking soda	8 mL
1 Tbsp.	ground cinnamon	15 mL
1 tsp.	salt	5 mL
2	eggs	2
½ cup	vegetable oil	125 mL
½ cup	apple juice	125 mL
¼ cup	honey	60 mL
1 cup	brown sugar, packed	250 mL
3	apples, peeled and grated	3
1½ cups	coarsely chopped dates	375 mL
1 cup	coarsely chopped pecans	250 mL

Grease a 10-inch (4 L) Bundt or tube pan, and set aside. Combine the flour, baking powder, baking soda, cinnamon and salt, and set aside. Beat the eggs until they are creamy and pale, add the oil in a slow, steady stream while beating. Add the apple juice, honey, brown sugar and apples. Mix well. Beat in the dry ingredients with a wooden spoon, then stir in the dates and pecans.

Spoon the mixture into the prepared pan, and bake at 375°F (190°C) until a toothpick inserted in the center comes out clean, about 50 minutes. Let cool for 10 minutes, then unmold.

Serves 4-6

CRÊPES

Crêpes are very thin French pancakes, not to be confused with our thick breakfast variety. Because crêpes freeze so well, I always have some on hand. Stuff with ham, leafy vegetables, mushrooms or cheese and cover with béchamel sauce for a nutritious light meal. With poached fruit, apple compote or ricotta cheese, crêpes become a scrumptious dessert.

3	eggs	3
1 Tbsp.	vegetable oil	15 mL
2 cups	milk	500 mL
	Pinch of salt	
1½ cups	all-purpose flour	375 mL
	FOR SWEET CRÊPES	
1 Tbsp.	vanilla extract	15 mL
2 Tbsp.	sugar	30 mL

In a large mixing bowl, beat together the eggs, oil and ½ cup (125 mL) milk (for sweet crêpes, add the vanilla extract and sugar as well). Add the salt and flour, alternating the flour with the remaining 1½ cups (375 mL) milk. Let stand for 2 hours.

The batter should lightly coat a spoon. If it is too thick, add a little water. Pour ¼ cup (60 mL) batter into a hot, lightly greased pan, tilting so that the batter spreads evenly to make thin pancakes. Cook until lightly browned, then flip, and briefly cook the other side.

Let the crêpes cool, then cover batches of 6 to 8 crêpes in plastic wrap, place in freezer bags, and freeze. Thaw in the refrigerator or at room temperature.

Makes about 3 dozen crêpes

CRÊPES WITH NECTARINES

If you use frozen crêpes and make the filling ahead of time, you can prepare this dessert in just a couple of minutes. Warm slightly in the microwave oven. You can also use peaches or apricots.

1 Tbsp.	butter	15 mL
4-5	nectarines, cubed	4-5
1 Tbsp.	honey	15 mL
1 tsp.	almond extract	5 mL
¼ cup	brown sugar	60 mL
4	crêpes (page 165)	4

In a heavy saucepan, melt the butter over medium-high heat, and cook the nectarines for 5 minutes. Add the honey, almond extract and brown sugar, and cook for 2 minutes.

Unfold 1 crêpe, and place one-quarter of the nectarine filling in the middle, fold the crêpe in half and again in half, or roll the crêpe, and place it on a serving plate. Repeat with the remaining 3 crêpes.

Serve the crêpes plain or with a dollop of sour cream.

Serves 4

SWEET POTATO GRATIN

This pudding is one of the delicious surprises of South American cuisine. It is equally good warm or cold.

2	eggs	2
¼ cup	butter, melted	60 mL
4 cups	grated sweet potatoes	1 L
2 cups	buttermilk or light cream	500 mL
1 tsp.	vanilla extract	5 mL
1 tsp.	grated orange peel	5 mL
½ tsp.	grated nutmeg	2 mL

In a large bowl, beat the eggs and butter. Add the remaining ingredients, and mix well. Pour into a greased shallow baking dish, preferably glass or ceramic. Bake at 350°F (180°C) for 1¼ to 1½ hours, until the top is golden brown and the center is firm to the touch.

Serves 6-8

BASIC PIE CRUST

For a crisp, flaky light crust, use cold butter and a chilled bowl and handle the dough as little as possible.

4 cups	all-purpose flour	1 L
1 tsp.	salt	5 mL
⅔ cup	cold butter	150 mL
⅔ cup	vegetable shortening	150 mL
1	egg	1
1 Tbsp.	vinegar	15 mL
¼ cup	cold water, or more	60 mL

Combine the flour and salt. Using two knives or a pastry cutter, cut in the butter and shortening until the mixture is the consistency of cornmeal. If using a food processor, whir the motor in pulses to achieve the same result. Add the egg and vinegar. Then add the water, 1 Tbsp. (15 mL) at a time, until the dough holds together but is not wet. Chill for 1 hour. Roll out the dough, and line pie plates.

Makes 3 medium pie shells

PARSNIP PIE

This is a modern version of a very old recipe from Kent, England, that dates back to the Middle Ages.

	Basic Pie Crust (page 171)	
3 cups	coarsely chopped, peeled parsnips	750 mL
¼ cup	honey	60 mL
1 tsp.	ground ginger	5 mL
½ tsp.	ground cinnamon	2 mL
½ tsp.	ground nutmeg	2 mL
2	egg yolks	2
	Grated peel and juice of 1 lemon	
	Pinch of salt	
1	egg, beaten	1
	Calendula petals (optional)	

Roll out the pastry dough, and line a 10-inch (25 cm) pie plate or flan tin. Trim the edges, and reserve the pastry cuttings.

Cook the parsnips in boiling water until soft (or steam if very young). Drain well, and mash thoroughly. Add the honey, ginger, cinnamon, nutmeg, egg yolks, lemon peel and juice and salt. Beat well, then spoon the mixture into the pie shell, and level the top with a spatula. Trim the reserved pastry cuttings to make a lattice pattern. Brush with beaten egg.

Bake at 400°F (200°C) for 30 to 35 minutes, until golden brown. Decorate with calendula petals, if desired.

Serves 4-6

LIGHT AMBERCUP CAKE

I like this cake plain—no frosting, no filling—so I bake it in a Bundt pan. But you can bake it in two 9-inch (1.5 L) round baking pans and make a layer cake using your favorite frosting.

⅔ cup	vegetable shortening	150 mL
1 cup	pureed cooked ambercup squash	250 mL
2	eggs	2
⅔ cup	maple or corn syrup	150 mL
2½ cups	all-purpose flour	625 mL
1 Tbsp.	baking powder	15 mL
1 tsp.	baking soda	5 mL
½ tsp.	ground cinnamon	2 mL
½ tsp.	salt	2 mL
½ cup	buttermilk	125 mL

Grease a 6-cup (1.5 L) Bundt pan or two 9-inch (23 cm) round molds, and set aside.

In a large bowl or in a food processor, beat together the shortening and the squash. Add the eggs, one at a time, while beating, then add the maple or corn syrup.

Combine the dry ingredients, and incorporate them into the squash mixture, alternating with the buttermilk. Spoon the mixture into the prepared pan(s), and bake at 375°F (190°C) for 30 minutes.

Unmold the cake, and let cool on a rack.

Serves 6-8

CORN AND SQUASH CAKE
WITH MAPLE-SYRUP SAUCE

The color of gold, this wonderfully moist cake can be made with any winter squash—
butternut, pumpkin or acorn.

3	eggs	3
½ cup	sugar	125 mL
1½ cups	pureed cooked squash	375 mL
	(see Note below)	
	Grated peel and juice of 1 orange	
1½ cups	corn flour	375 mL
1 tsp.	baking powder	5 mL
1 Tbsp.	orange blossom water (optional)	15 mL
	MAPLE-SYRUP SAUCE	
1 cup	heavy cream	250 mL
½ cup	maple syrup	125 mL
1 tsp.	maple extract (optional)	5 mL

With an electric mixer or a food processor, beat together the eggs, sugar and squash. Add the orange peel and juice, then the flour, baking powder and orange blossom water, if using. Beat well. Pour the batter into a greased shallow 8-by-8-inch (2 L) baking dish, and bake at 375°F (190°C) for 30 minutes (if using a glass baking dish, bake at 350°F/180°C and check regularly that the sides don't burn).

Meanwhile, make the sauce: In a small saucepan, combine the cream, maple syrup and maple extract, if using. Bring to a boil, and reduce the liquid over high heat until it is thick, about 5 minutes. Let cool.

Cut the cake into thick slices, top with maple-syrup sauce, and serve.

Serves 6-8

NOTE: To cook squash, peel, cut into chunks and steam for 15 minutes, or cook in the microwave oven on high for 3 to 5 minutes.

FRUITCAKE

Fragrant with rum and spices, studded with nuts and dried fruit, this fruitcake has a delightfully chewy texture. It freezes well and makes a great holiday gift.

1 cup	seedless raisins	250 mL
1 cup	chopped pitted dates	250 mL
1 cup	chopped dried figs	250 mL
½ cup	dark rum	125 mL
1 cup	unsalted butter, softened	250 mL
2 cups	brown sugar	500 mL
4	eggs	4
1 cup	finely grated butternut squash or carrots	250 mL
3 cups	all-purpose flour	750 mL
1 tsp.	each ground cinnamon, ground ginger and allspice	5 mL
1 tsp.	baking powder	5 mL
1 tsp.	baking soda	5 mL
½ tsp.	salt	2 mL
1 cup	buttermilk	250 mL
1 cup	chopped pecans	250 mL
1 cup	hazelnuts, skin removed	250 mL
½ cup	candied lemon peel	125 mL

Grease a 10-cup (2.5 L) Bundt or tube pan, and set aside.

Place the raisins, dates and figs in a bowl, add the rum, toss, and set aside.

Beat the butter with an electric mixer or in a food processor until creamy. Slowly add the sugar and eggs, one at a time, beating well after each addition. Beat in the squash or carrots.

Combine the flour with the cinnamon, ginger, allspice, baking powder, baking soda and salt. Stir the flour mixture into the egg mixture, alternating with the buttermilk. Add the rum-soaked fruit, pecans, hazelnuts and lemon peel. Mix well. Spoon the batter into the prepared pan, and bake at 325°F (160°C) until a toothpick inserted in the center comes out clean, about 1 hour. Let cool on a rack for 10 minutes, then unmold.

Serves 8-10

SCOTTISH OAT SCONES

In less than 30 minutes, you'll be enjoying these moist and crumbly scones.

1½ cups	all-purpose flour	375 mL
½ cup	quick-cooking rolled oats	125 mL
⅓ cup	sugar	75 mL
1 Tbsp.	baking powder	15 mL
	Pinch of salt	
⅓ cup	buttermilk	75 mL
⅓ cup	butter, melted	75 mL
1	large egg	1
½ cup	seedless raisins or dried cranberries	125 mL

TOPPING		
1 Tbsp.	sugar	15 mL
¼ tsp.	ground cinnamon	1 mL

Combine the flour, rolled oats, sugar, baking powder and salt in a medium bowl.

Beat together the buttermilk, butter and egg, and add to the dry ingredients. Mix until the dough binds together. Add the raisins or cranberries. Do not use a food processor, or the dough will be hard and chewy.

With floured hands, form the dough into a ball, and place it on a baking sheet lined with parchment paper. Pat out to form a 10-inch (25 cm) circle.

In a small dish, mix the sugar and cinnamon together. Sprinkle the topping over the dough. With a floured knife, cut the dough into 8 wedges, and spread slightly, leaving ⅛ inch (3 mm) between each piece.

Bake at 375°F (190°C) for 16 to 18 minutes, until light golden brown. Serve warm.

Makes 8 scones

INDEX